Embedded System Interfacing

Embedded System Interfacing

Design for the Internet-of-Things (IoT) and Cyber-Physical Systems (CPS)

Marilyn Wolf

MORGAN KAUFMANN PUBLISHERS

AN IMPRINT OF ELSEVIER

Morgan Kaufmann is an imprint of Elsevier
50 Hampshire Street, 5th Floor, Cambridge, MA 02139, United States

Library of Congress Cataloging-in-Publication Data
A catalog record for this book is available from the Library of Congress

British Library Cataloguing-in-Publication Data
A catalogue record for this book is available from the British Library

ISBN: 978-0-12-817402-9

For information on all Morgan Kaufmann publications visit our
website at https://www.elsevier.com/books-and-journals

Working together
to grow libraries in
developing countries

www.elsevier.com • www.bookaid.org

Publisher: Katey Birtcher
Acquisition Editor: Steve Merken
Editorial Project Manager: Susan Ikeda
Production Project Manager: Punithavathy Govindaradjane
Cover Designer: Christian Bilbow

Typeset by SPi Global, India

Contents

Contents

Preface

All computers need input and output to perform useful work. I/O systems are particularly important to embedded computers. While we may use standard devices in embedded systems, we often need to design specialized interfaces. Even when we do make use of standard devices, we need to be sure that the chosen interface meets the system's requirements. This book is dedicated to the art, science, and craft of embedded system interfacing.

I built my own Heathkit radios: a GR-64 shortwave receiver, an HD-10 electronic keyer, and an HW-16 novice transceiver. My friend Art Witulski and I tried to build a switch-based adder; we gave up when we realized that our PCB patterning technology far outpaced our soldering skills.

My hobbies and hanging around my Dad taught me a lot. My Stanford professors turned me into a competent electrical engineer. Let me pay homage to the professors who taught me about circuits over my 8 years there: Aldo Da Rosa, Robert Dutton, Umram Inan, Malcolm McWhorter, Ralph Smith, David Tuttle.

Perry Cook and I taught Pervasive Information Systems at Princeton for many years. We coached our students through the design of embedded systems. The term *Internet-of-Things* had not yet been coined but our students gained early exposure to many IoT concepts. Perry was the master hardware designer, building at one point an inductive coupler loop for a power plug to ensure that one student team did not electrocute themselves as part of their power line networking project.

But building your own electronics makes much less sense than it did a half-century ago. The decline of hand-built electronics in favor of highly integrated equipment has several causes: radios operate at much higher frequencies, many components are surface mount, integrated circuits provide much higher levels of integration. Integrated electronics are simply better than what you can design on a board: lower noise, lower distortion due to better matching, and lower power consumption.

Quite a few embedded interfacing books take the form of cookbooks—they provide example designs for particular applications. While cookbooks certainly have their place, I thought that a compendium of techniques was an important complement to the cookbook approach. The solutions found in a cookbook may not come with enough explanation to allow you to modify their design for your purposes. Principles help you understand how to make design decisions. Principles can help you modify an existing design or build a new design from scratch.

I ignored some of the traditional electrical engineering pedagogy in pursuit of my goal of a relatively short, stand-alone introduction to circuit design. I was not interested in the traditional passive/active circuit distinction; to some extent, I was not worried about digital versus analog. My guiding principle was function, moving from simple to complex. Logic is very simple in the sense that our set of values is limited; I also concentrated on the electrical characteristics of drive and load. Amplifiers simply change the power of a signal. Filters and detectors modify signals. Data conversion builds on these techniques to bridge the gap between analog and digital. Power also makes use of these circuit principles; a knowledge of circuit characteristics also help us to specify the important characteristics of power supplies.

Along the way, I emphasized a top-down approach. The specifications for a given function need to be clearly understood before we can design.

As I wrote, I realized that the critical decisions in interface design place two boundaries: the software/hardware boundary between software running on the CPU and the interface connected to the CPU, and the analog/digital boundary within the interface. The system specifications help to determine where to place these boundaries—a set of decisions for a high-speed, high-value system may not make sense for a simple consumer electronics device.

This book is designed as a *precis*, a short course in mixed-signal design. Consider this an outline of interesting and important topics. If you want to know more about a topic, dive in. The references provide some starting points on a number of topics; the Internet makes a wide variety of materials easily available.

Some of this technology has not changed since the 1970s and 1980s. In those cases, the oldies are still goodies. Here are some useful books:

- The *ARRL Handbook*, updated yearly, has been a go-to guide for all things EE for nearly a century.
- *Lancaster's Active Filter Cookbook* balances theory and practice for active filters. The book also provides a cornucopia of 1970's electronics, including biofeedback and psychedelic lighting.
- *IC Op-Amp Cookbook* by Walter G. Jung covers all aspects of linear and nonlinear op amp circuits.

In other cases, our techniques have changed profoundly. FPGAs have fundamentally changed our approach to logic design. Field-programmable analog arrays (FPAAs) have allowed microcontrollers to provide simple, integrated, configurable analog capabilities.

My Web site *marilynwolf.us* provides lab exercises that provide concrete forms of the exercises in this book. It also includes overheads for this material.

Many thanks to Prof. Robert Dick of the University of Michigan for his thorough and thoughtful comments.

Electronic design has given me a lifetime of pleasure. I hope you enjoy this pursuit as much as I have.

Marilyn Wolf, W2MCW
Atlanta, Georgia

CHAPTER 1

Introduction

1.1 Interfacing Computers to the Physical World

Useful computers need some sort of input and output. Computation that we can't see doesn't provide much attraction. Early computers used primitive I/O devices: lights, paper tape, crude displays. The development of new I/O devices has paralleled the development of CPUs.

I/O is particularly important to embedded computing systems. Embedded computers are responsible for a wide range of devices, ranging from simple appliances to complex vehicles and industrial equipment. This range of I/O requirements calls for a comprehensive playbook of interfacing techniques.

Embedded system interfacing is the conceptual interface between electrical and computer engineering—we require the skills of both fields to design good, practical interfaces. Computer engineers don't always have a lot of experience with traditional electrical engineering. As a result, we will cover this territory thoroughly. Readers with expertise in circuits should feel free to skip some sections and get straight to the use of circuits as interfaces to computers.

Embedded system interfacing is a good example of **mixed-signal design**—the design of circuits that combine analog and digital elements. Mixing analog and digital provides powerful capabilities but must be done carefully. Among other concerns, we must take care with the circuit characteristics of digital logic such as drive and load, something that is less of a problem in a purely digital design. Interfacing also requires **hardware/software codesign**, mixing the capabilities of software running on the CPU with mixed-signal circuits.

First, Section 1.2 surveys the goals of interface design and the techniques we use to achieve those goals. Section 1.3 surveys microprocessors. Section 1.4 signals introduces electrical signals. Sections 1.5 and 1.6 review the laws of electrical engineering: first for resistors, then generalizing to capacitors and inductors. Section 1.7 describes basic techniques for circuit analysis. Section 1.8 looks at nonlinear and active devices. Section 1.9 steps back to consider methodologies and tools for the design of interfaces. Section 1.10 walks through an outline of the remainder of the book. These sections will outline some basic concepts and terms in electrical engineering for later reference; we will flesh out these concepts as needed in later chapters.

Embedded System Interfacing. https://doi.org/10.1016/B978-0-12-817402-9.00001-7

1.2 Goals and Techniques

Embedded computer systems are used in all sorts of applications; one interesting way to think about the categories of embedded computers and their interfaces is the numbers of copies of the system that will be built. Experimenters and hobbyists build one system or perhaps a few. Industrial applications such as factories may build one-off devices but they also make use of specialized equipment that is manufactured at modest levels: hundreds to tens of thousands. Consumer products are manufactured in much larger volumes, from tens of thousands to tens of millions of units. Interface design skills are useful in all of these categories.

Many integrated circuits are *systems-on-chip* (*SoCs*) that include processing, I/O devices, and some amount of onboard memory. The design of these devices and their connections to the computing system is a critical aspect of the design of the SoC. While many SoCs do not include analog circuits, the digital devices must be designed with the characteristics of the analog devices to which they will be connected. Advanced packaging techniques allow the complete system to be composed of multiple chips built with different manufacturing technologies.

However, not all design is focused on integrated circuits. Many high-volume devices are built largely out of standard parts assembled on printed circuit boards—what engineers typically call **board-level design**. The printed circuit board also is a mainstay of industrial electronic design. A board design allows the design of a custom circuit with control over the components and manufacturing technology, all with substantially less cost and time commitment than is required to design an integrated circuit.

However, many designs require only a handful of the traditional primitives of electrical engineering: transistors, resistors, capacitors, inductors. Most board-level design puts together integrated circuits, each of which performs a specialized function. The op amp is a classic example of an integrated circuit that encapsulates a sophisticated circuit in an easy-to-use form.

While designing circuits using transistors is fun, it is often not realistic. Not only do integrated circuits save us time, but also they often provide better characteristics than circuits made from discrete components. But it is still important and useful to understand the basic principles of circuit design: we need to know how to evaluate the appropriateness of an integrated circuit for a particular application; and we need to be able to verify that we have designed the proper circuit connections to them. Providing insufficient current to the input of a logic gate, for example, will cause it to malfunction.

In order to design board-level systems properly, we need to be able to write the **specifications** for the design. We also need to understand the specifications of the components we use to build the board. These specifications are fundamental characteristics of circuits:

* Gain;
* Frequency response;

- Nonlinear characteristics such as rise time, ringing;
- Noise.

Design is the process of finding an embodiment of those specifications using available components. Circuit theory gives us important concepts in design:

- Drive and load;
- Filtering;
- Amplification gain and bandwidth.

We design the entire interface, which we often break down into smaller designs for the pieces of the interface. We use **top-down design** techniques to refine the specifications into realizations; **bottom-up design** methods allow us to estimate the characteristics of candidate designs.

We will see in Chapter 8 that an embedded system interface requires us to answer two questions:

- Where is the software/hardware boundary? What goes in software on the CPU and what goes into the interface?
- Where is the digital/analog boundary? What parts of the interface are performed with digital hardware and which with analog circuits?

1.3 Varieties of Microprocessors

A **microprocessor** is a CPU on an integrated circuit; in the modern era, virtually all CPUs are microprocessors. A computer system is more than a CPU—it requires memory, I/O devices, and interconnect between them. The term **platform** is often used to describe the complete computing hardware (and perhaps lower levels of the software stack as well). We often categorize platforms based on their size and complexity.

A **microcontroller** is a complete computer system on a chip: CPU, memory, I/O devices, and bus. We typically use this term for smaller systems: simpler CPUs, modest amounts of memory, and basic I/O. Many microcontrollers provide 4-bit or 8-bit CPUs; some of them provide less than a kilobyte of memory. The Cypress PSoC 5LP [16] is a microcontroller, although one with a 32-bit CPU. It provides an ARM Cortex-M3 CPU, three types of memory (flash, RAM, EPROM), and digital and analog peripherals.

A **digital signal processor (DSP)** is a microprocessor optimized for signal processing applications. The original use of the term referred to the combination of a hardware multiplier and Harvard-style separate program and data memories. Today, DSP optimizations include addressing modes useful for array calculations.

The term **system-on-chip (SoC)** is typically applied to more complex chips. Smartphone processors are a classic example of an SoC but complex platforms are built for a range of applications, including multimedia and automotive. The NXP S32V234 [46] is an SoC—a vision processor for automotive applications. It includes four ARM Cortex-A53 CPUs with SIMD instructions, two ARM Cortex-M4 CPUs, a vision accelerator, GPU, image sensor processor, image sensor interfaces, and support for safety and security.

1.4 Signals

A **signal** is a physical state over an extended period. We represent a signal mathematically as a value defined by a function over time.

We talk about signals with respect to their time values:

- DC (direct current) values do not change over time. Practically speaking, they change only slowly.
- AC (alternating current) values change over time. The term comes from sinusoidal signals but we apply it more generally to time-varying values.

We make this distinction because we use different techniques to analyze DC and AC signals and circuits. DC analysis makes use of simpler techniques.

AC signals can have arbitrary **waveforms** or shapes. For purposes of analysis, we deal with two major forms of signals. The sinusoidal signal is determined by its amplitude A, frequency ω, and phase φ:

$$v(t) = A \sin \omega t + \varphi. \tag{1.1}$$

The exponential signal is determined by its amplitude A and time constant τ:

$$v(t) = Ae^{-t/\tau}. \tag{1.2}$$

Fig. 1.1 shows examples of sinusoidal and exponential signals.

Noise is like weeds—any sort of undesired signal. Noise may come from random sources that we cannot predict or sources that we understand. When undesired signals come from predictable sources, we may use other terms, such as *interference* or *crosstalk*, to describe it.

We also talk about signals relative to the **domain** in which we view them:

- **Time-domain** signals are functions of time.
- **Frequency-domain** signals are functions of frequency.

These two representations are equivalent—we can transform a time-domain signal into its frequency-domain equivalent and vice versa. We can use the **Fourier transform** and its computational form the **fast Fourier transform** (**FFT**) to move between the time and frequency domains. Fig. 1.2 shows both representations of a signal which is formed by the product of two sinusoids, one fast and one slow. The frequency domain form shows the

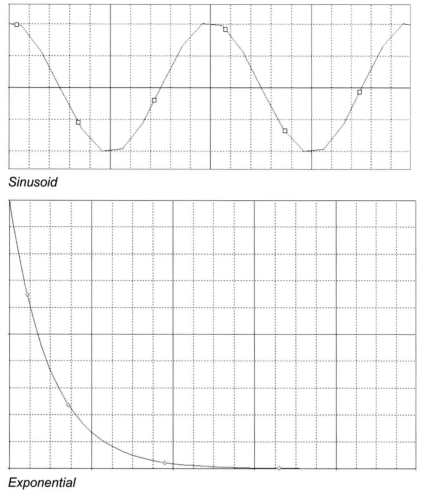

Sinusoid

Exponential

Fig. 1.1
Sinusoidal and exponential signals.

two sinusoidal components. (A frequency-domain signal includes both magnitude and phase components; we concentrate here on the magnitude part of the signal.)

Digital circuit designers rely almost exclusively on time-domain techniques—the nonlinear nature of digital circuits is not well suited to time-domain analysis. In contrast, linear circuits use both frequency-domain and time-domain methods; frequency-domain analysis is particularly useful for many aspects of linear circuit design. Fig. 1.2 shows examples of time and frequency representations of a simple signal.

We can refer to frequencies in either of two units: the variable ω is used for radians/s; the variable f is used for Hertz. By definition, 1 Hz $= 2\pi$ rad/s.

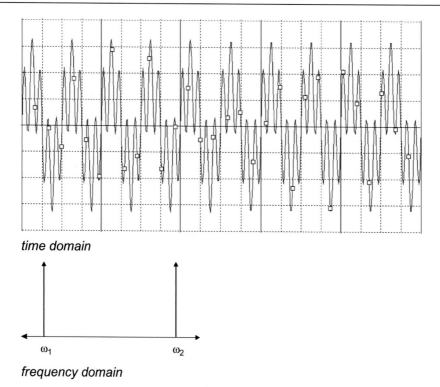

time domain

frequency domain

Fig. 1.2
Time- and frequency-domain representation of a signal.

Signals can traverse large dynamic ranges that result in some very large numbers. We can reduce the magnitude of our values by using **decibels (dB)**. This unit is one-tenth of a **Bel**, a unit of power named after Alexander Graham Bell. We can use decibels to express either ratios of values or to express a value relative to some reference. Since decibels refer to power, we should refer to voltage ratios as **dBV** although we often revert to using dB for these values as an abuse of notation.

Decibel curves are used to describe the response of filters and amplifiers. One common specification is the **half-power point**, also known as the **3 dB point** or the **corner frequency**, as shown in Fig. 1.3. The plot shows power as a function of frequency. The **Bode plot** method allows us to approximate frequency response curves using their asymptotes. The curve is defined by two asymptotes: a flat line to the left and a line descending at 20 dB per decade to the right; that rate is equal to 6 dB per octave. The point on the curve that is 3 dB below the left-hand asymptote has a power value 1/2 that of the asymptote. Since power is related to the square of voltage, the corresponding voltage has dropped by $1/\sqrt{2} = .7071$. We often refer to the half-power frequency as the **corner frequency**. We will discuss Bode plots in more detail in Section 5.4.

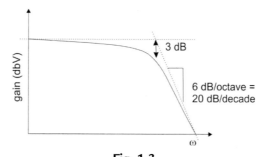

Fig. 1.3
The half-power point and cutoff frequencies.

1.5 Resistive Circuits

Electricity is a fundamental physical phenomenon. **Electrical engineering** (**EE**) is the study of techniques for the control of electricity (and, to some extent, magnetism).

EE is principally concerned with two physical quantities:

- **Electrical current**, commonly represented by the variable I.
- **Electrical potential**, also known as **voltage**, and represented by the variable V (or sometimes E for **electromotive force** or **EMF**).

Current is the macroscopic manifestation of the movement of electrons under the influence of an electrical potential. Electrons are always moving but, in isolation, their net movement is zero. An EMF results in a net movement of electrons which we can measure as current.

Ohm's law is one of the basic laws of electrical engineering:

$$V = IR. \tag{1.3}$$

The voltage across a device or region is proportional to the current flow through that device and its **resistance** R. The value of resistance is given in units of Ohms (Ω).

We sometimes prefer to work with conductance G:

$$G = {}^1/_R. \tag{1.4}$$

Conductance is given in units Siemens S.

Fig. 1.4 shows the voltage across and current through a resistor. Given Ohm's law, if we know the values of two of the system parameters $\{I, V, R\}$ we can determine the third.

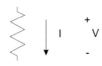

Fig. 1.4
Voltage and current in a resistor.

Two other laws describe the relationship between voltages and currents when we connect several resistors into **networks**. **Kirchoff's voltage law (KVL)** says that the sum of voltages around a loop is zero:

$$V_1 + \cdots V_n = 0. \tag{1.5}$$

Kirchoff's current law (KCL) states that the sum of currents into a node is zero:

$$I_{12} + \cdots I_{1n} = 0. \tag{1.6}$$

Fig. 1.5 gives an example circuit in the form of a graph: the nodes $\{1, 2, 3\}$ represent the points at which we evaluate Kirchoff's current law; the edges $\{12, 13, 23\}$ are where we evaluate Kirchoff's voltage law. We can define voltage variables along the edges and currents into or out of the nodes. When we make these labels, we choose which side or direction is positive and which is negative. So long as we are consistent in our labeling, the choice doesn't matter. The figure shows two **polarities** for the currents: $I_{13} = -I_{31}$ with the subscript gives the source and sink node for the current. In practice, we often choose a polarity for each current and give it a single subscript; we use the double-subscript notation here to emphasize the source and sink nodes for each current. We could also define reverse-polarity voltages across the resistors.

The voltages around the loop $\{V_{12}, V_{23}, V_{32}\}$ always sum to zero according to KVL. For any closed path through the circuit that does not repeat any circuit elements, $\sum V_{ij} = 0$.

The currents into each node always sum to zero thanks to KCL: for example, $I_{21} + I_{31} = 0$. When comparing the KCL equations for different nodes, we must be sure that the polarities are consistent between the nodes. Given a consistent labeling, we know that $\sum I_{ij} = 0$ for all the nodes in the circuit.

Thevenin's theorem of equivalence tells us that, given two nodes for which we can identify a voltage and current, we can find an equivalent network looking into those two nodes that

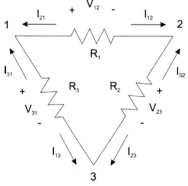

Fig. 1.5
An example of Kirchoff's voltage and current laws.

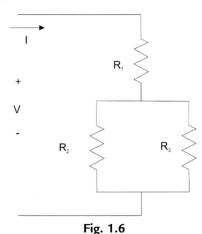

Fig. 1.6
An example of Thevenin equivalence.

consists of a voltage source in series with a resistor. In the example of Fig. 1.6, we can find the equivalent resistance of this network of three resistors. We first make use of the **parallel equivalence theorem** to reduce the parallel combination R_2, R_3:

$$R_{23} = {}^{1}\!\!\left/\left({}^{1}\!\!\left/_{R_2} + {}^{1}\!\!\left/_{R_3}\right)\right.\right.\!\!. \tag{1.7}$$

We then use the series equivalence theorem to reduce the series combination R_1, R_{23}:

$$R_{123} = R_1 + R_{23}. \tag{1.8}$$

The value R_{123} is the Thevenin equivalent resistance. **Norton's theorem of equivalence** provides the current source equivalent formulation of this transformation: a voltage source and resistor network can be represented as an ideal current source in parallel with a resistor. Fig. 1.7 shows the forms of the Thevenin and Norton equivalents.

1.6 Capacitive and Inductive Circuits

Capacitors and inductors are the other two basic electrical components. They share the common characteristic that their behavior depends on the frequency of the signal applied to them.

The current through a capacitor depends on the derivative of the voltage across the capacitor C:

$$I = C\frac{dV}{dt}. \tag{1.9}$$

Fig. 1.8 shows the current through and the voltage across a capacitor. At DC, $^{dV}\!/_{dt} = 0$ and no current flows—we say that the capacitor is an **open circuit** at DC. At infinitely high changes in voltage, the current through the capacitor is unlimited—it is a **short circuit** at high frequencies.

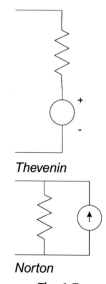

Thevenin

Norton

Fig. 1.7
Forms of the Thevenin and Norton equivalents.

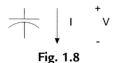

Fig. 1.8
Voltage and current through a capacitor.

The behavior of an inductor is complementary: its voltage depends on the derivative of the current through the inductor L:

$$V = L\frac{dI}{dt}.$$

(1.10)

Fig. 1.9 shows the current through and voltage across an inductor. The inductor is a short circuit at DC and an open circuit at high frequencies.

We can relate the behavior of these components more directly to a resistor by describing each as a **reactance** X which is a function of frequency ω, in units r/s (radians per second). The capacitor's reactance decreases with frequency:

Fig. 1.9
Voltage and current through an inductor.

$$X_C = \frac{1}{\omega C}. \tag{1.11}$$

Since $\omega = 2\pi f$, we can write this as

$$X_C = \frac{1}{2\pi f C}. \tag{1.12}$$

The inductor's reactance increases with frequency:

$$X_L = \omega L \tag{1.13}$$

or, in terms of Hertz,

$$X_L = 2\pi f L. \tag{1.14}$$

We use units of Ohms for reactance.

As will see shortly, we can create a uniform representation for both resistance and reactance known as impedance Z or its inverse, admittance Y.

1.7 Circuit Analysis

Impedance elements are **linear**—their behavior can be represented in the form $y = mx$. The graph of this function is a line through the origin with slope m. Although lines in general do not have to go through the origin, that property is critical to the notion of linearity in physical systems. We have also assumed that our circuits are **time-invariant**—the signals vary with time but not the component values. Systems that are **linear time-invariant** (**LTI**) obey superposition: their response to an input which is a sum of other inputs is the sum of the responses to the individual input components.

We have seen that we can write a set of equations for the voltages and currents in a circuit and solve for the unknowns. The form of the equations depends on the structure of the circuit and on the values of its components. When solving by hand, we generally use standard algebraic methods to manipulate and reduce the equations.

A more general approach is based on linear algebra. The **nodal analysis method** (also known as the **branch current method**) is particularly well suited to solution by a computer. It writes the branch currents in terms of the node voltages and the admittances of the devices:

$$I = YV. \tag{1.15}$$

$$\begin{bmatrix} i_1 \\ i_2 \\ \cdots \end{bmatrix} = \begin{bmatrix} Y_{11} & Y_{21} & \cdots \\ Y_{12} & Y_{22} & \\ \vdots & & \ddots \end{bmatrix} \begin{bmatrix} v_1 \\ v_2 \\ \cdots \end{bmatrix}. \tag{1.16}$$

Given the voltages, we can solve for the currents. For a purely resistive circuit, these equations are simple. When the circuit includes reactive components, the system of equations includes differential or integral equations.

We also need more abstract representations of circuits and signals than are provided by nodal analysis and Kirchoff's laws. We can use the **Laplace transform** to translate the differential equations into the **s domain** and simplify analysis. The s parameter is complex with $s = \sigma \pm j\omega$. (We traditionally write the imaginary number as j to avoid confusion with current.) The Laplace transform integrates with an exponential:

$$F(s) = \int_0^\infty e^{-st} f(t) dt. \tag{1.17}$$

Many operations are easier to perform in the s domain; we can invert the transformation back into the time domain when we are done. The frequency-dependence reactance formulas of Eqs. 1.11 and 1.13 are special cases of the s domain.

We can combine s domain impedances using the series and parallel equivalences:

$$Z_{ser}(s) = Z_1(s) + Z_2(s). \tag{1.18}$$

$$Z_{par}(s) = \frac{1}{\frac{1}{Z_1(s)} + \frac{1}{Z_2(s)}}. \tag{1.19}$$

We use voltage sources to describe the initial condition of capacitors and current sources for the initial condition of inductors; each has its own representation in the s domain. We can solve for the variable of interest in the s domain and then use inverse transforms to translate back into the time domain. The s-domain form of impedances allows us to algebraically manipulate resistances and reactances uniformly.

The **impulse response** is another key description of its behavior. An impulse $\delta(t)$ has a duration of zero time and it has unbounded value over that time; the integral of the impulse over all time is 1:

$$\int_{-\infty}^\infty \delta(t) dt = 1. \tag{1.20}$$

The impulse response is interesting in itself—ringing a bell is a practical example of an impulse response. But we are also interested in the impulse response because we can derive the circuit's response to other forms of input from its impulse response.

The **order** of a circuit or its functional model is given by the number of energy storing devices in the circuit. A **first-order** impulse response has the form (given here using voltage variables):

$$V(t) = V(0)e^{-t/\tau} + V_f. \tag{1.21}$$

$V(0)$ is the value of the response at $t=0$ while V_f is the final value. τ is known as the **time constant** and is a function of the circuit components. In the case of an RC circuit, $\tau = RC$. Fig. 1.10 shows an example of a first-order exponential response. In this case, $V_f = 0$; we can estimate τ from the graph by finding the time on the vertical axis at which $V = V(0)e^{-1}$ and reading off the horizontal axis value $t = \tau$.

A **second-order** circuit response, illustrated in Fig. 1.11, can take one of three cases depending on the relative values of the circuit components. The overdamped case is the sum of two exponentials:

$$V(t) = V_1 e^{s_1 t} + V_2 e^{s_2 t}. \tag{1.22}$$

The two roots of the response s_1, s_2 are both real-valued, for example, $s_1 = 0.1$ s, $s_2 = 0.02$ s. This form of response resembles the first-order case.

The underdamped case is the sum of two damped exponentials:

$$V(t) = V_1 e^{-\sigma t} \cos \omega t + V_2 e^{-\sigma t} \sin \omega t. \tag{1.23}$$

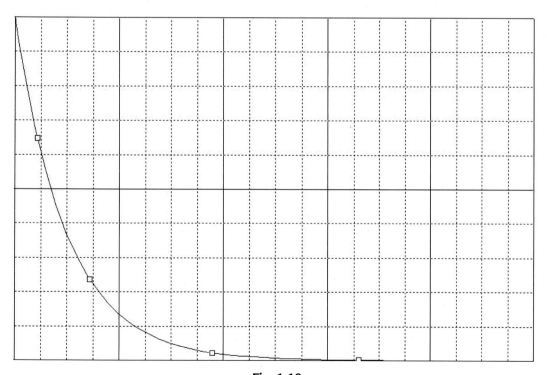

Fig. 1.10
Impulse response of a first-order system.

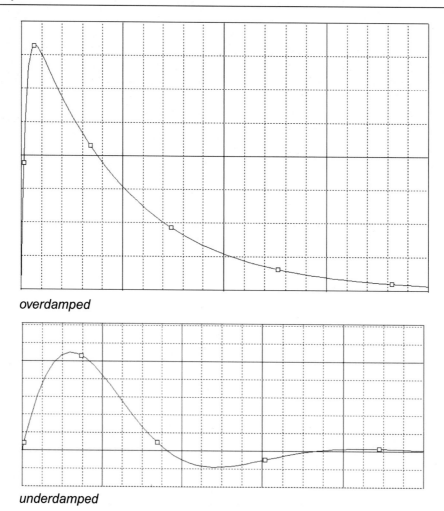

overdamped

underdamped

Fig. 1.11
Overdamped and underdamped responses of second-order systems.

The two response values are complex conjugates: $s = \sigma \pm j\omega$. This response is very different from the first-order case—the response rises and falls around the steady-state value.

The critically damped case has the same form as the overdamped case but the two roots are identical.

1.8 Nonlinear and Active Devices

We are very interested in devices that are **nonlinear**: diodes, transistors, etc. The nonlinearity of diodes can be used for decisions, such as whether a given voltage represents a logic 0 or 1.

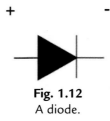

Fig. 1.12
A diode.

Fig. 1.12 shows the schematic symbol for a standard pn diode. When a positive voltage is applied above a certain level, the current through the device is effectively that of a short circuit. When a reverse voltage is applied, the diode is effectively an open circuit. Several other types of diodes exist with specialized properties, such as operating at different voltages, emitting light, or detecting light.

We are also extremely interested in devices—transistors, primarily—that are **active**. Resistors, capacitors, and inductors are all **passive** because they cannot amplify signals. Transistors, in contrast, provide amplification, which conveys a number of important advantages.

Fig. 1.13 shows two common transistor types. The **MOSFET** (metal oxide semiconductor field-effect transistor) is used for both digital and analog circuits. This symbol is for a particular type of MOSFET, *enhancement mode n-type*. The current between the source and drain

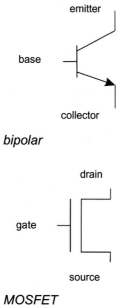

Fig. 1.13
MOSFET and bipolar transistors.

terminals depends on the voltage at the gate. The **bipolar transistor** used to be widely used for both digital and analog circuits; today, it is primarily used for analog applications. The emitter-collector current is a function of the base current. In both cases, one signal can be used to control another, stronger signal. MOSFETs and bipolar transistors differ in several important ways that we will study in succeeding chapters.

Both MOSFETs and bipolar transistors can be considered at least roughly linear over a portion of their range; that linearity is used to build many types of amplifiers. However, their nonlinear characteristic cannot be ignored and they complicate the solution of the circuit equations. Circuit simulators use iterative methods to evaluate the behavior of circuits with nonlinear devices. The simulator alternates between using an estimate of the node voltages and branch currents to estimate the state of the nonlinear device, then using the device values to update the voltages and currents. Each evaluation, known as a **time step**, stops when the differences between successive sets of values become sufficiently small.

1.9 Design Methodologies and Tools

Ultimately, we need to move beyond circuit theory to the design of useful interfaces. A **design methodology** is a sequence of steps we perform during design. Some parts of the methodology will be automated while others will be manual.

We start with a set of loosely formulated **requirements** for the interface. We then refine those requirements into a **specification** that includes specific values and other details of what the interface should do.

Analysis is an important first step. We may propose some rough designs and then use our analytic tools—Kirchoff's laws, s domain analysis, etc.—to characterize the design and to select some component values. Most of our analysis will be done by hand.

Simulation complements analysis. Simulators can analyze circuits, particularly nonlinear circuits, much more accurately than we can do by hand. Simulators can also be given a long list of input signals to help us better understand the design space. Digital logic simulation is usually done with hardware description languages (HDLs) such as Verilog or VHDL. The HDL description is fed to a simulator, which then provides waveform or tabular outputs.

The basic procedure is similar for analog circuits but with graphical input of the circuits. Fig. 1.14 shows a simple circuit for analog simulation. The circuit is entered using a **schematic capture** tool that is linked to a circuit simulator. We will use the OrCAD schematic capture tool and *Pspice* simulator throughout this book to demonstrate sample designs.

Simulating our design before we build it helps to minimize the chance of expensive and time-consuming mistakes. Some aspects of interface design are hard to simulate without expensive setups—simulating the interaction between CPU software, digital logic, and analog circuits requires a sophisticated simulator. But simulating key parts of our design using

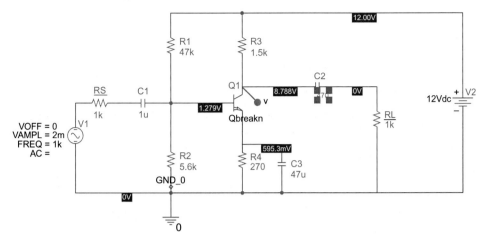

Fig. 1.14
A circuit design for simulation.

either digital or analog simulators can build confidence in the design before we buy parts and spend time building.

At some point, we have created our design: analog circuits, digital logic, software. Unless we are very experienced, we probably want to *prototype* our design to be sure it is up to snuff. Prototyping helps us ensure that the boundaries between the computer and the circuits are properly designed. Prototyping also lets us evaluate the characteristics of the circuit. While we may be able to perform simple tests of the interface without the microcontroller, we need to connect the interface to the microcontroller to fully test the system. Modern manufacturing techniques rely on advanced packages for integrated circuits that are difficult to work with manually. We typically use an **evaluation board** for the microcontroller we have chosen. Fig. 1.15 shows an evaluation board including a microcontroller, support logic, and switches and buttons; the rear of the board includes sockets where **daughter cards** can be attached. Fig. 1.16 shows an evaluation board with a **prototyping module**; small components can be plugged into this area, wired together, and connected to the microcontroller's inputs and outputs.

We also need some sort of equipment to test the circuit and understand what it is doing. Given the relatively slow frequencies at which many interfaces operate, relatively inexpensive equipment often works fine. A simple voltmeter allows us to test voltages around the circuit. Inexpensive *oscilloscopes* connect to a PC for their user interface; these instruments often include several channels of *logic analyzer* for digital signals.

If we only need one copy of the interface, we may be done. If we want to build multiple copies, we probably want to move beyond prototyping techniques to some form of *manufacturing*. **Printed circuit boards (PCBs)** can be manufactured in very small quantities at reasonable costs. PCBs also provide much better characteristics than do prototyping-style wiring.

Chapter 8 will also discuss prototyping and manufacturing technologies for embedded systems.

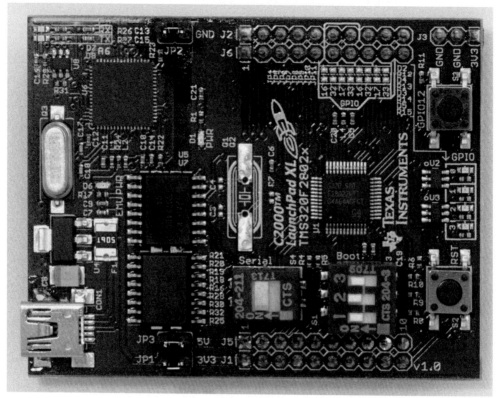

Fig. 1.15
An evaluation board.

1.10 How to Read This Book

In the rest of this book, we will develop techniques for designing interfaces: we will start with subsystems and move onto complete interfaces. The chapters combine analysis with practical examples. Here is a summary of the remaining chapters:

- Chapter 2 studies several types of standard interfaces. Many common interfaces, such as I^2C or USB, are based on defined, published standards and have many commercial embodiments. Understanding how they work can help us to understand the role of interfaces in embedded systems as well as provide practical techniques.
- Chapter 3 concentrates on digital logic interfaces. We will look at both the logical design of basic interfaces as well as their circuit characteristics. When designing logic in an FPGA, for example, we can often ignore circuit issues because our primitives are designed to be compatible. Compatibility is not assured when we mix and match logic from several different sources or when we connect analog and digital circuits. When designing interfaces, we have to be sure that our digital logic obeys basic circuit principles—if not, the interface may not behave in its properly logical manner.

Fig. 1.16
An evaluation board with a prototyping area.

- Chapter 4 studies on amplification using transistors. Amplification is a key operation in all sorts of interfaces. Some basic principles will allow us to design and build amplifiers suited to our particular requirements.
- Chapter 5 considers filtering, signal generation, and detection. Filtering is a critical complement to amplification. We can filter using both analog and digital techniques, each with its own advantages. We make use of several different types of controlled, precision waveforms: sine waves, square waves, etc. We may want to generate a signal directly for output; we may also use generated signals to control other parts of our interface. Detecting signals is a nonlinear operation that complements filtering.
- Chapter 6 studies circuits that convert between analog and digital representations. Conversion is at the heart of interfacing. We need to understand how converters work in order to apply them properly and choose the best type for our application.
- Chapter 7 looks at power delivery and conversion. Real circuits do not provide ideal power sources. We need to understand the limitations of realistic power circuits and their effects on both analog and digital circuits. Studying the design of power conversion circuits helps us understand what they do; in some cases, we may want to design our own as well.

- Chapter 8 puts together these techniques to create mixed-signal systems that combine analog and digital systems. Mixed-signal design is the heart of interfacing. It requires us to deploy all of our design skills, both analog and digital.

The body of the book emphasizes MOSFETs. Two appendices concentrate on bipolar devices and circuits:

- Appendix A describes TTL logic.
- Appendix B analyzes bipolar amplifiers.

Please don't limit your reading of this book to these pages. The book Web site contains additional material. A set of presentations summarizes the material in this book. Lab exercises complement and extend the descriptions in this text. Lab procedures can change, particularly where software is involved; the Web site provides a forum for sharing updated materials.

Questions

Q1.1   Find the equivalent resistance of these circuits:

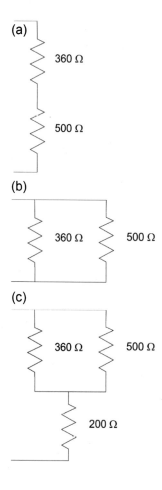

Q1.2 Find an equivalent impedance for each circuit:

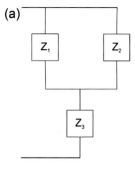

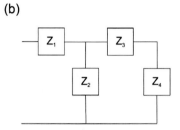

Q1.3 This circuit is known as a **voltage divider**:

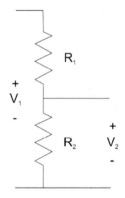

What is the ratio V_2/V_1 given R_1, R_2?

Q1.4 You are given this **bridge circuit**:

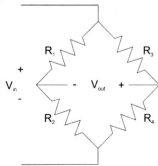

Find V_{out} as a function of V_{in}.

Q1.5   Plot the reactance of a capacitor with $C=1$ µF over the range $[628, 6.28 \times 10^6]$ r/s.

Q1.6   Plot the reactance of an inductor with $L=1$ mH over the range $[628, 6.28 \times 10^6]$ r/s.

Q1.7   Plot the impedance of these circuits over a range $[20, 20 \times 10^6]$ Hz:

    (a)   Series $R=1$ kΩ, $C=1$ µF

    (b)   Series $L=1$ mH, $C=1$ µF

    (c)   Series $R=1$ kΩ, $L=1$ mH, $C=1$ µF

Q1.8   For each of these ladder circuits, find the s-domain transfer function $T(s) = V_{out}(s) / V_{in}(s)$ in terms of the Z impedances:

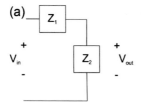

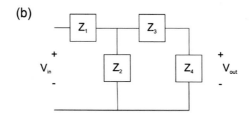

Q1.9   For each transfer function, draw a pole-zero diagram:

(a) $\dfrac{1}{(s-j10^3)(s+j10^3)}$

(b) $\dfrac{s^2}{(s-j10^3)(s+j10^3)}$

CHAPTER 2

Standard Interfaces

2.1 Introduction

A number of interfacing standards are in daily use. Standards such as I^{2}C or USB have been built into many components and systems. Typically, using them requires no hardware design and limited software design. Understanding how these interfaces work is very useful. Their principles also help us understand the role of interfaces in embedded systems.

Fig. 2.1
The **Open Systems Interconnection (OSI)** model.

The **Open Systems Interconnection (OSI)** model, shown in Fig. 2.1 is widely used to describe the design of computer networks. The model includes several layers that start at the most basic physical characteristics at layer 1 up to the application in layer 7. This chapter concentrates on the bottom three layers, known as the media layers:

- Layer 1, the **physical layer (PHY)**, includes the physical and electrical characteristics of the connection. Physical characteristics include, for example, the type of connector used. Electrical characteristics describe the signals used for data.
- Layer 2, the **data link layer**, describes the basic transfer of data from one network node to another. The unit of transfer at this level is the frame. This layer is divided into two sublayers. This layer is divided into two sublayers: the **media access control (MAC)** layer controls how devices can gain access to the communications medium; the **logical link control (LLC)** layer identifies and encapsulate protocols at the network layer as well as managing error correction and frame synchronization.

Embedded System Interfacing. https://doi.org/10.1016/B978-0-12-817402-9.00002-9

23

- Layer 3, the **network layer**, moves data sequences from one node to another, potentially across several different types of networks.

In this chapter, we will look at six different standard interfaces:

- The **RS-232 serial interface** commonly used on personal computers.
- The **I²C interface** which is used to communicate with devices along a relatively simple bus; we also discuss the **I²S bus** used for digital audio and the **CAN** bus used in automotive systems.
- The **Universal Serial Bus** (**USB**), which has gone through several revisions as a common standard for PC interfacing.
- **WiFi**, a wireless network widely used for PCs and also for IoT systems.
- **Zigbee**, a wireless network designed for embedded systems.
- Two wireless interfaces, **Bluetooth** and **Bluetooth Low Energy** (**BLE**). Despite sharing a common root name, these two interfaces vary in some interesting and important ways.
- **LoRaWAN**, a low power wide area network.

In Section 2.9, we will consider Internet connections that rely on communications interfaces.

2.2 RS-232

Serial interfaces are some of the oldest computer interfaces, predating many features of modern computer systems, including the OSI model. A number of different serial interfaces and protocols have been defined over the years. The **RS-232** standard was created in 1960 and was provided on most personal computers for many years. Today, few PCs provide a serial port but RS-232 is still used in some types of industrial equipment. Serial ports do not run at high speeds by modern standards but their hardware and software requirements are both minimal.

Fig. 2.2 shows a typical early use case for RS-232 connections; this configuration helps explain some of the terminology used in the standard. When a computer was the size of a room, users often sat elsewhere and connected to the computer over serial lines. Modems were used to transmit data over the phone line. RS-232 links were used to connect the modems to the computer and terminal, respectively. In this scenario, the terminal is data terminal equipment (DTE) and the modem is data circuit-terminating equipment (DCE).

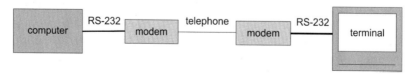

Fig. 2.2
A typical early use of RS-232.

The RS-232 electrical standard uses much higher voltages than are typically used today. Those high voltages often require specialized circuits; however, they do provide some amount of resistance to noise in challenging environments. The standard allows signals of up to 25 V; both positive and negative voltages are used and voltages around ground are not valid levels. The mark data signal is sent as a low voltage level while the space is a high voltage level.

Fig. 2.3 shows the 9-pin D-sub connector used for serial ports. This connector is an example of the mechanical specification required for interfacing—users must be able to plug into the connector. The nine pins are used for various signals:

- Pin 1: data carrier detect (DCD).
- Pin 2: serial data input (RxD).
- Pin 3: serial data output (TxD).
- Pin 4: data terminal ready (DTR).
- Pin 5: ground (GND).
- Pin 6: data set ready (DSR).
- Pin 7: request to send (RTS).
- Pin 8: clear to send (CTS).
- Pin 9: ring indicator (RI).

TxD and RxD are the data transmit and receive lines, respectively. These directions are defined from the terminal or computer: transmit goes from a terminal to a modem, for example. A **null modem** is a device with two connectors that swaps the transmit and receive lines from one connector to the other.

Fig. 2.4 character shows the form of a character on an RS-232 connection. Transmit and receive rates are controlled by their own clocks; these clocks are considerably slower than the clocks used in typical logic. A character starts with a start bit, which is always a low voltage and lasts for one bit period. Data bits follow, followed by a parity bit. The character ends with a stop bit, which is at least the length of one bit and may last up to two bits.

Parity provides simple error detection. A parity bit is added to the character; the value of the parity bit depends on the bits in the character. First, we perform the exclusive-OR of all

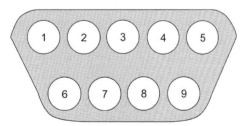

Fig. 2.3
A D-sub connector used for RS-232.

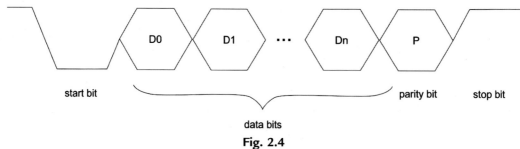

Fig. 2.4
A transmitted RS-232 character.

the character bits. We then have two possible protocols to follow: **even parity** sets the parity bit so that the exclusive-OR of the data plus parity bits is even (0); **odd parity** sets the parity bit to give an odd result (1). The receiver can compute the exclusive-OR of the bits it received; it has earlier agreed on the even/odd protocol to be used. If the parity of the received character does not match the specified parity, the receiver can signal an error.

We can study the 8251A data sheet to understand the RS-232 signals. A few terms are useful. **Baud** rate is the rate at which symbols are sent; the bit rate is the rate at which bit values are transmitted. If the communications medium can encode more than one symbol in a bit, then the bit rate is higher than the baud rate. **Mark** and **space** are used to describe logic 1s and 0, respectively. A typical RS-232 connection would include a computer one end, a terminal on the other, and a modem in between.

DSR' is the logically inverted form of data set ready provided by the 8251. The CPU can test this signal to determine if the modem is ready to operate. DTR' is also logically inverted; it indicates whether the terminal is ready.

The roles of RTS and CTS have changed over time. Originally, they were used to switch the direction of data; the relatively simple modems of the time could move data in only one direction over time. Eventually, modems became more sophisticated and devices became able to send larger blocks of data. As a result, RTS and CTS became used for **flow control**. A flow control protocol, shown in Fig. 2.5, is a form of *handshaking* that is used to manage rates and avoid overrunning buffers. The transmitter and receiver are each controlled by their own state machine; the interaction between these state machines defines the protocol. The transmitter responds to an internal *go* signal to start the transmission process. It sends an RTS signal high and waits for the receiver to return with CTS. It sends the required data bits; when it is done, it deasserts RTS (i.e., sets RTS low), then waits for the receiver to deassert CTS. The receiver runs concurrently. When it receives an RTS, it waits for an internal OK signal before signaling, using the CTS signal, that it is ready to receive. It receives bits, then expects the transmitter to deassert RTS, at which point it deasserts CTS. Each side of the transaction has moved through its four states to return to the initial state, leaving each side ready for another character. The ready to receive (RTR) signal found in later versions of the RS-232

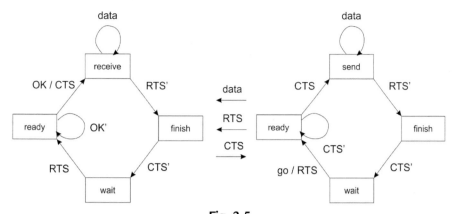

Fig. 2.5
Transmit and receive state machines for flow control.

standard shares the same pin as RTS but are used for this flow control operation. The ring indicator signal can be used by the modem to tell the terminal or computer that the phone line is ringing. The C/D line is used to indicate whether the bus contains data or a command.

One common way to build an RS-232 interface is by using particular chip, the Intel **8251A**. The 8251A design was later offered by other manufacturers as its popularity spread. The 8251A was designed to be able to implement a number of existing serial communication standards; it is flexible but the designer was largely responsible for harnessing that flexibility into a usable serial link.

Fig. 2.6 shows a block diagram of the signals on the 8251A. The signals on the left side go to the computer while those on the right side go to the serial line. Several of these CPU signals correspond to RS-232 signals: DSR, DTR, CTS, and RTS are all given in negative form. Data is

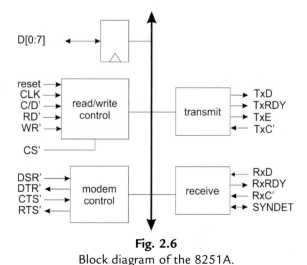

Fig. 2.6
Block diagram of the 8251A.

supplied on eight parallel, bidirectional lines. The C/D' signal is used to determine whether the data lines represent data (0) or control (1) information. The reset signal allows the chip to be reset. CLK provides the clock. RD' and WR' are used to tell the 8251A that the CPU is reading or writing words. On the serial line side, we have transmitted serial signals. TxD is transmitting data, TxRDY signals whether the transmitter is ready, TxE signals that the transmitter has no characters ready to send. TxC' is a clock used to determine the rate of the data symbols. RxD is the receive data, RxRDY indicates that the receiver is ready, RxC' is the receive data clock. The SYNDET/BRKDET signal is used as either an output (sync detect) or an input (break detect).

The 8251A has seven internal eight-bit registers. Two of the registers—the transmit and receive buffers—are used for the data that is transmitted or received. The sync1 and 2 characters are used in synchronous mode only. The status register gives status and error information. The mode register determines whether synchronous or asynchronous mode will be used along with their parameters. The command register is used for enabling, disabling, and error handling.

After the 8251A is reset, the CPU needs to send two words: first, a mode instruction which specifies synchronous or asynchronous along with some operating parameters; next, a command instruction which sets up the transmit and receive modes.

The mode instruction bits are used as follows:

- Bits 0-1 specify the baud rate factor: synchronous mode (00), 1X (01), 16X (10), or 64X (11). This factor determines the conversion rate between the mark/space rates and the transmit or receive clocks.
- Bits 2-3 specify the character length: 5 (00), 6 (01), 7 (10), or 8 (11) bits.
- Bits 4-5 specify parity: even (11), odd (00), or disabled (10, 01).
- Bits 6-7 specify the length of the stop bit: 1 (01), 1.5 (10), or 2 (10).

The command register bits include:

- Bit 0, TXEN, enables (1) or disables (0) the transmitter.
- Bit 1, DTR sends an nDTR output value in negated form (1 for 0, 0 for 1).
- Bit 2, RXE, enables (1) or disables (0) the transmitter.
- Bit 3, SBRK, sends a break character (1) or specifies normal operation (0).
- Bit 4, ER, sets (1) or keeps (0) error flags.
- Bit 5, RTS, sets an nRTS value in negated form.
- Bit 6, IR, performs an internal reset (1) or normal operation (0).
- Bit 7, EH, enables hunt mode (1), or normal operation.

The status bits include:

- Bit 0, TXRDY, signals whether the transmitter is busy (0) or ready (1).
- Bit 1, RXRDY, signals whether the receiver is busy (0) or ready (1).

- Bit 2, TXEMPTY, indicates whether the transmitter is busy (0) or done (1).
- Bit 3, PE, indicates a parity error (1) or OK (0).
- Bit 4, OE, indicates an overrun error (1) or OK (0).
- Bit 5, FE, indicates a frame error (1) or OK (0).
- Bit 6, SYNDET, indicates whether a sync char was detected (1).
- Bit 7, DSR, indicates the DSR value in negated form.

One of the charms of RS-232 is that it is slow and simple enough that we can watch it operate. A breakout box is a simple device with a pair of D-sub connectors. The RS-232 signals flow through but they are also shown on LEDs. The data is usually too fast to read directly but the control signals can be seen; watching them allows us to see how the serial line is operating.

2.3 I^2C, CAN, and I^2S

I^2C [45] is widely used to connect multiple chips in systems. The bus provides relatively low data rates, so its uses are primarily for mode control and similarly low-speed uses. However, its extremely low cost has helped to make it ubiquitous. The **CAN** bus [8] is widely used in automotive electrical and electronics (EE) systems. Its structure is very similar to I^2C.

The physical layers of I^2C are very simple. As shown in Fig. 2.7, the serial bus includes two wires: **serial data (SDA)** and **serial clock (SCL)**. Each line is connected to a **pullup resistor**. When a device wants to send a zero on either wire, it turns on a transistor to pull down the wire. When no device wants to transmit a zero, the pullup resistor ensures that the wire's value remains high. This arrangement ensures that conditions which cause two devices to try to write at the same time do not damage the bus; it also ensures that the bus signal always carries a valid logic value. The standard provides for several modes that run at different rates: 100 kbit/s for standard mode, 400 kbit/s for fast mode, 1 Mbit/s in fast mode plus, and 3.4 Mbit/s in high speed mode. The logic levels for standard mode put $-0.5 \text{ V} \leq V_{IL} \leq 0.3 \text{ V}$, $V_{IH} \geq 0.7 \text{ V}$. The standard move allows for a maximum clock frequency of 100 kHz.

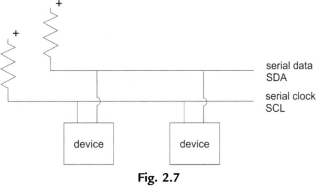

Fig. 2.7
Physical design of the I2C bus.

The CAN bus uses a similar physical layer that can transmit at 1 Mb/s over a maximum length of 50 m; a variation using an optical link has also been developed.

All data is sent as eight-bit bytes. As shown in Fig. 2.8, the data is transmitted from most-significant bit (MSB) to least-significant bit (LSB). The receiving slave acknowledges each bite: the master temporarily releases SDA; the slave pulls SDA low for an acknowledgment or leaves it high for a negative acknowledgment.

As shown in Fig. 2.9, a data transfer consists of a start bit, a sequence of bytes, and a final stop bit. A start bit is signaled by a high-to-low transition on SDA while a stop bit is signaled by a low-to-high transition on SDA. The first part of the data transfer is the address, plus a read/write bit. This figure shows the original 7-bit address mode: the first seven bits of the first byte are address, with the eighth bit indicating read/write'. A 10-bit address mode uses the first two bytes for address and read/write'; the high-order five bits of the high address byte are 11,110. A master can generate successive data transfers by sending another start signal without having sent a stop; this feature allows the master to send to several different slaves without the overhead of intermediate stop bits.

Because the bus may have more than one master, mastership must be **arbitrated** to determine who can transmit. Unlike some busses, arbitration occurs during the transmission of the address bit. The protocol takes advantage of the physical layer design to simplify arbitration. A device may start to write when the bus is inactive. When two devices try to write at the same time, each cannot tell that another device is trying to transmit until the two devices try to send different bits. Both devices monitor the bus as they transmit. When they detect a conflict, the device with the lower priority immediately stops transmitting. The bus clock is slow enough that the valid bit can be properly transmitted during the remainder of the clock period. The standard reserves some addresses, including a general call address. Sending a general call, followed by a second byte value of 00000110 signals a software reset. CAN uses a similar arbitration method. Nodes listen to the bus to determine when a new transmission begins.

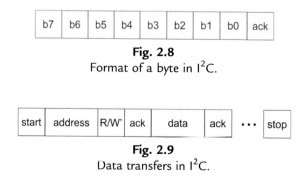

Fig. 2.8
Format of a byte in I^{2}C.

Fig. 2.9
Data transfers in I^{2}C.

Devices typically come from the manufacturer with a default address. Some devices do not allow the address to be changed at all; others allow a limited range of address reprogramming; some allow for arbitrary reprogramming of the address. If the device does not provide for sufficient address reprogramming, a common solution is to assign each device a unique identifier in the data section of the device. Each data transfer to this class of device starts with the device address, followed by a byte which gives the identifier for which the transfer is intended. This solution comes at the cost of bus bandwidth.

The **I²S** bus [47] has a very similar name and was developed by the same company but is used for very different purposes. This bus is one of several designed solely as a streaming audio interface for communication between chips in consumer audio systems. The bus includes three lines: clock SCK, word select WS, and data SD. Word select is used to indicate whether the data is for the left or right channels, implicitly limiting the standard to stereo. Any device that drives the clock effectively serves as master but the standard provides no mechanism for switching between bus masters.

2.4 USB

The **Universal Serial Bus**, more commonly known as **USB**, is used in billions of computing devices. Given its ubiquity in computing, it should be no surprise that it is used for embedded system interfacing, either to connect to a host PC or to connect the embedded computer to other devices.

USB [14, 26] has evolved over several versions over the past two decades, offering higher performance and other features over time. USB 1.1 ran at 12 Mbit/s, USB 2.0 at 480 Mbit/s, USB 3.0 at 5 Gbit/s, USB 3.1 at 10 Gbit/s, and USB 3.2 at 20 Gbit/s.

From the point of view of applications running on the USB **host**, the devices on a USB bus provide **functions** to applications on the host. As shown in Fig. 2.10, each application deals with a function; it does not see the bus as a whole. The applications use USB application

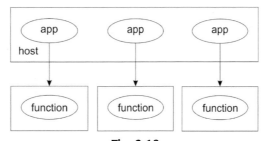

Fig. 2.10
Applications and functions in USB.

programming interfaces (APIs) to deal with the functions, not low-level device operations. We will discuss USB APIs in more detail later.

Physically, a USB bus is a tree as shown in Fig. 2.11. The host provides the **root hub** for the network; the host interface is known as the **Host Controller**. The root hub connects to one or more **hubs** which then connect to some combination of devices or other hubs. The bus may have at most seven tiers of devices, including the root hub. Logically, the USB bus appears as a bus—all devices and hubs see the same data traffic. However, the SuperSpeed connections in USB 3.x are not shared but rather point to point.

USB 2.0 uses a four-wire cable to connect the nodes of the network: a power signal V_{bus}, ground, and two data lines D+ and D−. A clock is encoded along with the data. Differential signaling is used to improve noise immunity. The data signals use nonreturn to zero inverted (NRZI) encoding: no change in the signals indicates a 1 while a change indicates a 0. A clock can be extracted from the data stream at each end of the connection by monitoring the transitions. However, a long string of 1 s would result in no transitions, leaving the circuits no information from which to infer the clock. This problem is solved by *bit stuffing*: a zero is inserted after every string of six consecutive 1 s. The stuffed bit is then removed by the receiver. The Enhanced SuperSpeed USB 3.1 architecture adds four more lines for the high-speed data which flows separately from the low/full/high-speed data provided by USB 2.0. Data on the SuperSpeed path is encoded using an 8b/10/b encoding while SuperSpeedPlus uses a 128/132b encoding; these encodings provide a more sophisticated form of transition management for clock recovery.

Functions may be self-powered or draw power from USB. As the standard has grown, the power delivery capabilities of a connection have grown from relatively modest to very

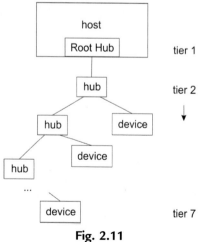

Fig. 2.11
The structure of a USB bus.

substantial: 0.5 W for USB 1.0, 2.5 W for USB 2.0, and 100 W in the new USB Power Delivery specification. (USB 2.0 did allow for a charging downstream port that was not compliant with the standard but could supply more power.) Enhanced SuperSpeed provides additional power management capabilities. Because the SuperSpeed data is routed to its destination, not broadcast, devices that are not the target of the communication can remain in a low-power state.

Fig. 2.12 shows the layer diagram for the host and device sides of a USB bus. On the host side, the client application logically interacts with the device's function layer. The host's USB system software layer and the USB logical device layer provide functions to perform the necessary operations on the host and device sides, respectively. The USB host controller and USB bus interface are physically connected on the USB bus to perform the required communication.

The host controller initiates all transfers. The bus protocol is based on polling. The protocol used to connect between the host and a function endpoint is known as a **pipe**. Pipes can be one of several types:

- **Stream pipes** flow data from source to destination. The order of bytes is maintained and no structure is imposed by USB.
- **Message pipes** operate on a request/data/status model and provide bidirectional communication.

A *message pipe* has a well-defined structure; a *stream pipe* does not. Pipes can be configured with bandwidth, transfer service type, and endpoint characteristics.

A device presents a set of **endpoints** to the host, each of which is a destination for communication. An endpoint provides several parameters to the application software to manage communication: endpoint number, bus access frequency and latency requirements,

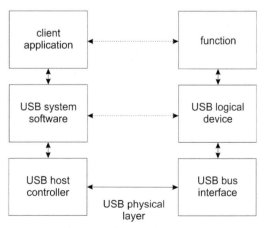

Fig. 2.12
Layer diagram for USB host and device.

required bandwidth, maximum packet size, error handling, transfer type, direction of transfer. The Default Control Pipe is required to be endpoint zero on each device; it is used in status and control.

Transfers are one of four types:

- **Control transfers** are host initiated and used for status queries and commands.
- **Isochronous transfers** are periodic, streaming transfers.
- **Interrupt transfers** provide bounded-latency communication and are intended to be used infrequently.
- **Bulk transfers** are nonperiodic and intended for large data transfers that are not time sensitive.

If a device requires several different types of connections, each is established in a different pipe.

Communication on the bus is structured into *packets*. Bits are sent on the bus least-significant bit first; bytes are sent in little-endian order with the LSB first. A packet includes a SYNC field, a *packet identifier (PID)*, a function address field, an endpoint field, a frame number field, a data field of length ranging from zero to 1024 bytes, and *cyclic redundancy checks (CRCs)* for tokens and data. A PID may be of one of four types: token, data, handshake, or special. Each type is subdivided into categories. Data is divided into frames or microframes in USB 2.0. A frame is marked by a Start-of-Frame (SOF) token on the bus. At full speed, SOF tokens are generated at 1 ms intervals; at high speed, they are generated at 125 µs intervals. Frame numbers are used to identify frames or microframes. A separate packet format is used for Enhanced SuperSpeed USB.

USB supports split transactions which separate the request from the response. Split transactions allow other devices to use the bus while the request is being processed.

A device can be in one of several states:

- A device enters the *attached* state when it is connected to the USB bus.
- When power is applied to the device, it is in the *powered* state.
- When the device has been reset, it is in the *default* state.
- Once an address has been assigned to the device by the Host Controller, it is in the *address* state.
- After other required configuration operations have been performed, the device is in the *configured state*.
- A device may be *suspended*, in which case the host may not use its function.

When a device is attached to the bus, the Host Controller **enumerates** the device:

- The Host Controller receives an event on its status change pipe. The device is in the attachcd state.

- The host queries the hub to determine the nature of the change and identify the port being used.
- The host then waits for at least 100 ms as the device powers up. The device is in the powered state.
- The host issues a reset command to the port. The device is in the default state.
- The host uses the Default Control Pipe to determine the device's maximum data payload.
- The host assigns a unique address to the device, putting the device in the address state.
- The host reads the possible configurations of the device; it may have more than one possible configuration.
- The host determines a configuration value for the device, based on the device's possible configurations and how it will be used. Once the device has finished its configuration process, it is in the configured state.

In addition to their particular functions, each USB device must provide several common operations:

- Dynamic attachment and removal at any time.
- Address assignment.
- Configuration.
- Data transfer.
- Power management.
- Power budgeting—the configuration process selects the power mode for the device in part based on the available power on the bus, given the power needs of other devices.
- Remote wakeup to take a device out of its suspend state.
- Request processing.

USB imposes some timing limits on operations: 5 s to process a command, 10 ms recover time between attachment to the bus and starting transfers; 50 ms for the Status stage of setting an address and 2 ms for recovery after setting the address; 50 ms for the Status stage of a device request with no Data stage; 500 ms to start data transfers for a request with data.

A hub connects one upstream port with several downstream ports. A hub includes of three major subsystems: the *Hub Controller*, the *Hub Repeater*, and the *Transaction Translator*.

The host is responsible for detecting when devices are attached and removed, managing control and data flow to and from the devices, collecting status and activity statistics, and providing power. These services are managed by the **USB System Software** which has three components: the *Host Controller Driver*, the *USB Driver*, and the *Host Software* or application. The Host Controller performs several types of operations:

- Management and reporting of its own state.
- Serializing output data and deserializing input data.
- Generation of microframes.

- Managing data requests to and from the host.
- Performing the USB protocol operations.
- Detecting and reacting to error messages.
- Place the bus into a Suspended state and be able to wake up the bus.
- Perform Root Hub functions.
- Provide a Host System Interface.

2.5 WiFi

WiFi is the brand name for a set of wireless data standards. The standards are part of the IEEE 802.11 family. This set of standards defines MAC and PHY for wireless local area networks; the standards operate over several bands. Data rates depend on the member of the family; examples include at 6–54 Mbits/s and 802.11n at 54–600 Mbits/s.

Data is organized into frames consisting of a MAC header, payload, and frame check sequence. Management frames are used for maintenance operations.

WiFi was created for fixed and mobile computing applications which generally operate at higher power levels than do modern Internet-of-Things devices. Techniques have been developed to reduce the power consumption of WiFi for use in embedded applications.

2.6 Zigbee

Zigbee is a network- and application-level wireless standard. It makes use of PHY and MAC layers from the IEEE 802.15.4 standard. It provides data rates of up to 250 kbits/s.

Each Zigbee network has one Zigbee Coordinator (ZC) to form the root of the network. A Zigbee End Device (ZED) provides only basic functionality and cannot send or receive directly with other devices. A Zigbee Router (ZR) passes data between devices and/or the coordinator; it can also run applications. A network can run in either a beacon or beaconless mode. If operating in beacon-enabled mode, routers periodically transmit; devices may turn off in between beacon transmissions to save energy.

Zigbee adds two layers above the PHY and MAC layers supplied by 802.15.4: network data service (NWK) and application (APS). The PHY layer operates on *packets* while the MAC layer operates on *frames*.

The network layer provides data and management. The network layer ***discovers*** nodes in the network. It forms a network: it identifies a channel on which it can operate; it then assigns a 16-bit network address to each device in the network. Communication may be broadcast, multicast, or unicast. A network may be organized as a tree or a mesh. The network layer limits the number of hops, known as the **radius**, across which a frame may travel. The network layer is responsible for discovering routes through the network and building a routing table. After formation of the network, the coordinator manages the process of devices joining or leaving the network.

The application layer includes three major components. The application support (APS) sublayer interfaces to the network layer. The Zigbee Device Object (ZDO) is responsible for device management and services, including defining whether it operates as coordinator, router, or device. ZDO also manages security operations.

The application framework provides several services, including a message service for data transfers and a key-value pairs (KVPs) for service attributes. **Application profiles** can be used to manage the configuration of application; several profiles for common applications have been defined. A profile is named by a 16-bit profile identifier which must be issued by the Zigbee Alliance. A profile includes clusters and device descriptions. A cluster has its own 16-bit identifier; it consists of a set of attributes organized as key-value pairs. The clusters are used to organize the attributes. The device description is kept separate from the application profile itself. It consists of five components: the node descriptor (type, manufacturer code); power (battery powered or wall powered, battery state); simple descriptor (profile identifier, clusters); complex descriptor (serial number, etc.); and a user descriptor of up to 16 ASCII characters for additional information.

Security is based on AES 128-bit keys. Master keys are preinstalled into a trust center which then provides keys to other nodes in the network for secure communications.

2.7 Bluetooth and Bluetooth Low Energy

Bluetooth [23] was developed in the mid-to-late 1990s for applications such as telephony and PC device operation.

The physical layer operates on the Industrial-Scientific-Medical (ISM) band, a radio frequency band that is allocated globally for license-free operation. Data is modulated using frequency-hop spread spectrum, which changes frequencies according to a schedule in order to both improve security and reduce interference. Hops are performed at a rate of 1600 hops/s. The interval between hops defines a *slot* during which one packet can be transmitted. Packets have a fixed format, including an access code, packet header, and data payload of up to 2745 bits. Multislot packets can also be sent using up to five slots. It offers a peak data rate of 1 Mbit/s.

Bluetooth supports two types of links:

• **Synchronous connection-oriented (SCO)** links provide symmetrical, streaming links for services such as voice.

- **Asynchronous connectionless (ACL)** links are designed for bursty transmissions; they can operate either symmetrically or asymmetrically.

Establishing a connection between devices is known as **pairing**.

Bluetooth devices can organize ad hoc networks known as **piconets**. One device, usually the device that set up the network, operates as the master. The master coordinates frequency hopping by transmitting a master clock.

Bluetooth systems can be divided into a controller, host, and applications. The controller includes several layers:

- The physical layer provides the radio and air interface.
- Direct test mode can be used to test the physical layer.
- The link layer provides data link services.
- The host/controller interface (HCI) is the interface to the host.

The host includes:

- The **logical link control and adaptation protocol (L2CAP)** provides a channel abstraction and multiplexes channels onto the data link.
- The security manager manages pairing and key distribution.
- The **attribute protoco**l defines the data access on peer devices.
- The **generic attribute profile** defines attributes types and their use.
- The **generic access profile** defines discovery and connection services.

The application layer defines several components:

- **Characteristics** are data in a known format and a universally unique identifier (UUID).
- **A service is a set of characteristics and their associated behavior.**
- **Profiles** describe the use of services.

Bluetooth Low Energy (BLE) is defined under the Bluetooth umbrella but it differs in many ways. BLE has been optimized for low energy operation, which means in part using the radio as little as possible. BLE devices are **stateful**—they maintain state between radio operations. BLE operations are **connectionless**, a significant change from classic Bluetooth. BLE is organized as a *client–server* system. It provides a **service-oriented architecture** to access information on the server.

2.8 LoRaWAN

Internet-of-Things applications have motivated the design of new networks designed to cover large geographic areas but still provide low-power operation for battery-powered devices. LoRaWAN [35] is an example of such a network. The network makes use of spread spectrum techniques. Communications can be set to various data rates; the network server manages the data rate and radio power of the link for both battery life and available bandwidth. Data rates may fall between 0.3 and 50 kbits/s. LoRaWAN is designed for much longer range operation than is typical for wireless networks. A LoRaWAN link can operate over a mile (2 km) in urban environments with a great deal of interference and over 10 miles (20 km) in areas with low interference.

A LoRaWAN device operates in one of three classes. A Class A device communicates only when initiated by the end device; all communication is asynchronous using the Aloha protocol. A Class B device synchronizes to network beacons; synchronization can reduce latency at the cost of higher power consumption. A Class C device keeps its receiver on at all times, providing lower latency for downlink transmissions but resulting in higher power consumption.

A LoRa gateway connects to a set of devices in a star architecture; the gateway is connected to the Internet and translates data between the LoRaWAN link and the Internet. The network defines both network session keys and application session keys based on the AES standard.

2.9 Internet-Enabled Devices

Internet-enabled devices are used in all sorts of applications and at almost every level of system complexity. The design of an Internet-enabled device requires us to span the software/hardware boundary.

The **Internet Protocol (IP)** was developed to provide **internetworking** communications. Early computer communications networks were islands; multiple standards complicated efforts to build large-scale networks. The Internet Protocol allows data to be moved across networking boundaries in a consistent manner. A number of services have been built on top of IP:

- The **Transmission Control Protocol (TCP)** augments IP by providing error correction, ensuring end-to-end delivery, and allowing recipients to reconstruct the order of data spread across multiple packets. TCP operates at layer 4 and provides connection-oriented service.
- The **User Datagram Protocol (UDP)** is a connectionless service for datagrams.
- The **Hypertext Transfer Protocol (HTTP)** provides request-response service for distributed applications with the World Wide Web as a classic example.

The Internet Protocol can be performed on a wide range of communications media. The higher-level, host-oriented operations are generally performed in software. The choice of media for an Internet-enabled device can take into account a number of considerations:

- Communications bandwidth.
- CPU resources required.

- Cost and physical size.
- Power consumption.
- Compatibility with available communication networks.

Design of an Internet-enabled device also needs to consider the relationship between networking and applications. Few applications will directly make use of IP. Higher-level protocols provide useful distributed services in a standard way. The **publish/subscribe** design pattern is widely used for IoT systems. The publishers in the system generate messages but do not specify particular recipients. Subscribers can identify what types of messages are of interest to them. Brokers are typically used to decide which messages should be sent to each subscriber. The publish/subscribe model allows easy entry and exit of nodes in the system; many IoT systems allow nodes to enter and exit the network at will.

Several different protocols are used to build IoT devices. HTTP is often used to provide device-oriented services and simple device interfaces. CoAP [28] provides stateless HTTP transfers and is designed for use on IoT devices. MQTT [27] is an IoT-oriented protocol based on a publish/subscribe model. It can operate on TCP/IP; it can also run on other protocols that provide connections that are ordered (data can be reassembled in the order in which it was transmitted), lossless (data may be retransmitted until it is received at the destination), and bidirectional. MQTT was designed as an alternative to HTTP for IoT applications: MQTT uses a simpler data model that does not introduce document-oriented concepts; MQTT clients do not need to know what devices receive their data, thanks to the publish/subscribe model; MQTT is simpler than HTPP, with fewer operations as well smaller and simpler messages; MQTT provides quality-of-service (QoS) levels; and the MQTT publish/subscribe model provides multipoint communication.

Questions

Q2.1   Compare and contrast PHY, LLC, and MAC layer roles in the OSI model.

Q2.2   Compare bandwidth of I^2C in standard mode and USB 3.0.

Q2.3   Compare the physical layer network topologies of I^2C and USB 3.0.

Q2.4   What is the purpose of device enumeration in USB?

Q2.5   Compare bandwidth of WiFi 802.11a, Zigbee, Bluetooth.

Q2.6   How do the network behaviors of devices on Bluetooth and BLE differ?

Q2.7   Describe the roles of the major components in a publish/subscribe system.

CHAPTER 3

Logic

3.1 Introduction

Logic design is a critical component in embedded interfaces. When we design logic using components that have been designed to work together, we can concentrate on their logical function. But interfacing often requires us to mix and match components, exposing incompatibilities. In these cases, an understanding of the circuit characteristics of logic is essential to ensuring that the logic works as intended.

The next section discusses specifications for digital logic. Section 3.3 introduces CMOS logic, based on MOSFETs, and its circuit characteristics. Section 3.4 introduces the high-impedance output gate. Section 3.5 looks at two structures for busses: open drain and high impedance. Section 3.6 discusses registers used to hold state. Section 3.7 examines programmable logic devices. Section 3.8 looks at logic structures we use to connect to CPUs. Section 3.9 discusses steps we must take to protect logic circuits from both electrostatic discharge and noise. Section 3.10 discusses common auxiliary devices such as LEDs. Section 3.11 designs a simple shaft encoder.

3.2 Digital Logic Specifications

The most basic specification for a digital logic circuit is its logical function. Function is specified as Boolean formulas in the case of combinational circuits—logic with no internal state. A state transition diagram or register-transfers can be used to specify sequential machines.

However, a practical digital logic circuit must meet other specifications. Those nonfunctional specifications are the primary concern of this chapter.

Timing is a key parameter for interface logic—the interface may not produce the right functional result if its logic does not meet certain timing parameters. Timing parameters come in several forms:

- Delay from a specified input to a specified output.
- Relative timing from one signal event to another signal event.

Bus operations are often specified using timing diagrams as shown in Fig. 3.1. Signals in the timing diagram may be given either as absolute values or as stable/changing regions.

Embedded System Interfacing. https://doi.org/10.1016/B978-0-12-817402-9.00003-0
41

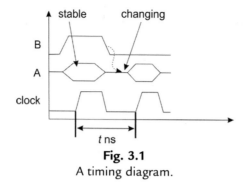

Fig. 3.1
A timing diagram.

The arrows in the timing diagram specify **timing constraints**—one event must occur before another. If an event is labeled with a time value, the second event must occur at least that period of time after the first event. We will study some important timing parameters for registers in Section 3.6.

Logic signal levels are also related to the proper functioning of logic. Some logic families define signal requirements relative to voltages, others to currents. If the input to a logic gate does not meet the required signal levels, the gate will not produce the correct logical output signal. We will study logic signal levels in Section 3.3.

Power consumption is often specified as a maximum value. The logic must live within the available power from the power supply.

3.3 CMOS Logic Circuits

A **logic family** is a circuit technology that can be used to create many different types of gates: inverter, NAND, NOR, etc. Most logic today is based on CMOS logic families based on MOSFETs.

Fig. 3.2 shows two types of CMOS transistors. CMOS transistors are MOSFETs; the C stands for *complementary*. The two types of transistors provide opposite polarities: when a gate voltage is applied, it enables current to flow between the source and drain. The n-type transistor conducts when its gate voltage is positive while the p-type transistor conducts on a negative gate voltage. Both of these devices are known as enhancement mode because current increases with larger gate voltages. (Depletion mode transistors conduct less current as their gate voltage increases. Some logic families use depletion transistors but standard CMOS uses only enhancement devices.) The gate terminal is capacitive and has a high input impedance.

The **characteristic curve** plot of Fig. 3.3 shows the drain current as a function of drain-source voltage for several different gate-substrate voltages. At each gate voltage, no current flows below a threshold voltage. When the gate voltage crosses the threshold, the drain current

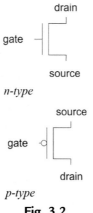

Fig. 3.2
CMOS transistors.

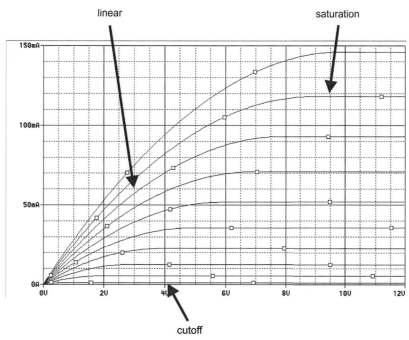

Fig. 3.3
Characteristic curves of an nMOS transistor.

increases in the linear region until it peaks in the saturation region. We will study MOSFET characteristics in more detail in Chapter 4.

Logic gates are amplifiers but highly nonlinear ones. We will discuss linear amplifiers in Chapter 4, which we use for amplifying signals while preserving their details. Logic gates are designed to provide reliable digital values by taking advantage of nonlinearity.

Fig. 3.4 shows the schematic for a CMOS inverter built from one n-type (the **pulldown** M_2) and one p-type (the **pullup**, M_1) transistor. The schematic also shows a capacitor connected to its output as a load. The input is connected to the gates of both transistors. (Unfortunately, we use gate to refer both to a logic gate and a transistor gate.) The source of each transistor is attached to a power supply terminal, VSS for the n-type and VDD for the p-type. The gate voltage is measured relative to that power supply level. When a high voltage is applied to the input, M_2 is on (high Vgs) and the p-type is off (low Vgs). As a result, M_2 discharges the load capacitor. If a low voltage is applied to the input, M_2 is off and M_1 is on, charging the load capacitor.

Given this basic understanding of how these logic families work, we can set up a scenario in which each logic families fail. CMOS is sensitive to **fanout**—the number of gates attached to the output of a driver gate. Fig. 3.5 shows a NAND gate whose output is connected to three other gates; this connection is sometimes called a **fanout tree**. The mechanisms by which they fail are different thanks to the different operating characteristics of the families. **Fanin** is the number of gates connected to the input of a given gate; some logic families are also sensitive to fanin constraints.

Capacitance is at the root of the fanout problem. In practice, the load capacitance is the gate capacitance of the transistors that form the next logic gate. As fanout increases, the capacitive load increases. As shown in Fig. 3.6, we can model this situation with a current source for the driver gate's output and a capacitance for the load. One of the driver gate's transistors is on and

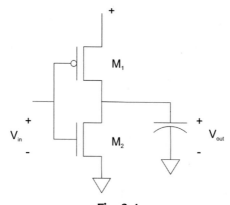

Fig. 3.4
A CMOS inverter.

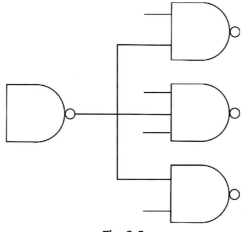

Fig. 3.5
Fanout of a gate.

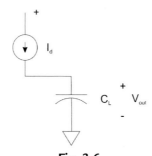

Fig. 3.6
A model for fanout in CMOS logic.

operates in its saturation region. The input capacitances of the load gates are in parallel so we can add them to find the total load capacitance. The voltage across this capacitance is equal to the input voltage at each fanout gate; all fanout gates see the same input voltage. That voltage waveform is simple—a ramp until it reaches the power supply voltage, at which point the driver transistor turns off. The slope of the ramp depends on the ratio of the load capacitance and the driver current:

$$V_{out} = I_d C_{out} t, V_{out} \le V_{DD} \qquad (3.1)$$

The output current is determined by the logic family. As the load capacitance increases, the slope decreases and the time required for the voltage to reach its final value increases. Interfaces have timing requirements—a maximum delay from the change of an input to the change at its output. If the slope of the voltage waveform is shallow enough, the logic fails to satisfy its timing requirement.

Given these illustrations of the importance of electrical specifications to the proper function of logic gates, we can now look at the specifications themselves. Most logic families represent logic values as voltages; a few logic families use currents to represent logical values. We talk informally about a high voltage representing a logic 1 and a low voltage representing a logic 0. In fact, a range of voltages can be used to represent logic values. Accepting a range of signal values protects the logic functions against noise, which is inevitable in real circuits. Intermediate values represent invalid logic values, which we often refer to as X. Leaving a gap between the valid logic 0 and logic 1 levels also contributes to **noise immunity**. Without an X value in between, a small amount of logic would flip the logical value. If noise pushes a valid logic value into the X range, we can at least detect that the value is invalid.

The **data sheet** for each component is a critical part of your design: without a data sheet, you don't know the component's characteristics. The data sheet for a logic gate or family specifies characteristics of input and output signals: for input signals, the required voltages and currents to signal a valid logic value; for output signals, guarantees on the signals that the output generates. Fig. 3.7 illustrates the relationships between logic levels when one gate drives another. The highest voltage that represents a logic 0 is V_{OL}; the lowest input voltage that represents a logic 0 is V_{IL}. If $V_{IL} < V_{OL}$, we know that any valid logic 0 produced by the output gate will be interpreted as a logic 0 by the next gate. Similarly, if $V_{OH} > V_{IH}$, we are guaranteed that any logic 1 produced by the output gate will be treated as a logic 1 by the input gate. The high and low ranges do not have to be the same and the input and output ranges do not have to be equal.

Fig. 3.8 shows some of the specifications from a data sheet for a CMOS NAND gate. CMOS logic can operate over a wide range of voltages. The input voltages V_{IL}, V_{IH} and the output currents I_{OL}, I_{OH} are both specified. CMOS output voltages asymptotically approach the power supply voltages so their worst-case levels do not need to be specified.

If we mix logic from two different logic families, we need to be careful to obey the input and output signal specifications. These specifications also limit our ability to connect logic gates to nonlogic circuits. For example, a logic gate may not be able to supply enough current to directly drive a speaker.

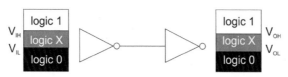

Fig. 3.7
Logic levels and logic gates.

V_{CC}	$3\,V \leq V_{CC} \leq 5.5\,V$
V_{IH}	$V_{CC} = 3\,V: V_{IH} = 2.1\,V$ $V_{CC} = 4.5\,V: V_{IH} = 3.15\,V$ $V_{CC} = 5.5\,V: V_{IH} = 3.85\,V$
V_{IL}	$V_{CC} = 3\,V: V_{IL} = 0.9\,V$ $V_{CC} = 4.5\,V: V_{IL} = 1.35\,V$ $V_{CC} = 5.5\,V: V_{IL} = 1.65\,V$
I_{OH}	$V_{CC} = 3\,V: I_{OH} = -4\,mA$ $V_{CC} = 4.5\,V: I_{OH} = -24\,mA$ $V_{CC} = 5.5\,V: I_{OH} = -24\,mA$
I_{OL}	$V_{CC} = 3\,V: I_{OH} = -4\,mA$ $V_{CC} = 4.5\,V: I_{OH} = -24\,mA$ $V_{CC} = 5.5\,V: I_{OH} = -24\,mA$

Fig. 3.8
Selected data sheet entries for a CMOS logic gate [62].

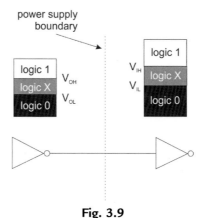

Fig. 3.9
Signal level incompatibilities across power supply boundaries.

If we mix logic that operates at different power supply levels, we also need to be careful about signal levels. Many digital systems use multiple power supply voltages, which they use to trade off power consumption and performance. Since the range of valid logic 0 and 1 voltages depends on the power supply voltage, changing power supply levels leads to changing the range of valid logic values. As illustrated in Fig. 3.9, if we connect the output of a gate at a low power supply voltage to the input of another gate at a higher power supply voltage, a voltage produced by the first gate as a logic 1 may be too low to be interpreted as a 1 by the next gate; instead, it could be treated as a logic X.

3.4 High-Impedance and Open-Drain Outputs

Some logic gates offer another form of output, known as high impedance, three-stating, or tri-stating™. Three states are useful in connecting gates together to form a bus. Fig. 3.10 shows two three-state gates connected to a bus. Each gate has its data input as well as an enable input: if enable $=1$, the gate's output is the inverse of the data input; if enable $=0$, the gate's

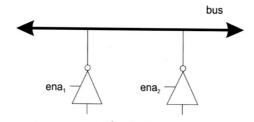

Fig. 3.10
Common connections using three-state logic outputs.

output is set to high impedance. We often refer to the high impedance output value as **Z**. We can select which gate writes its value on the bus by setting the values of the two enable inputs. Of course, if both gates are enabled, they will both be electrically connected, which is particularly bad when the data values are different. Not only can this cause a bad logical value to appear on the bus but it may damage the circuits due to large short circuit currents.

Fig. 3.11 shows a CMOS inverter with a three-state output. The inverter's output is guarded by n-type and p-type transistors M_3, M_4. When enable$=0$ (and enable'$=1$), both of these transistors are off, defeating both M_1 and M_2. When enable$=1$ and enable'$=0$, both transistors are on and the pullup and pulldown transistors can effectively determine the proper output value.

Some logic families do not include a pullup device or resistor. Instead, the bus or external connection is connected to a pullup resistor R_1 as illustrated in Fig. 3.12. Pulldown transistors inside the gates will, when turned on, cause the bus voltage to go low. If no gate tries to pull the

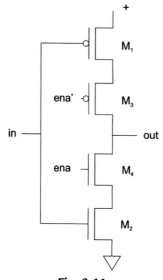

Fig. 3.11
A CMOS inverter with three-state output.

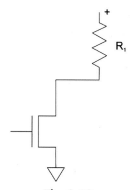

Fig. 3.12
An open-drain bus circuit.

bus voltage down, the pullup maintains the bus at a high logic level. The MOS version of this circuit is known as **open drain** since the transistors' drain connections are left unconnected.

In the case of TTL, this configuration is known as **open collector**. The maximum current supplied by the pullup resistor must be no larger than the maximum sink current of one gate and the current flowing from the inputs of the n fanout gates [58]:

$$R_L \geq \frac{V_{CC} - V_{OL,max}}{I_{OL} - nI_{IL}} \tag{3.2}$$

3.5 Example: Open-Drain and High-Impedance Busses

Busses are common connections that are used for data communication between various combinations of devices. Only one device at a time may write the bus. The destination for the data may be one or several devices. We can use two different circuit families to design busses with different characteristics.

We can use **pullup resistors** to build busses that allow easy connection and disconnection of devices. If the transistors used on the bus are bipolar, we refer to the bus as **open collector**; if the transistors are MOSFETs, the bus is **open drain**. A classic example of the open-drain/open-collector bus is I^2C, which we discussed in Section 2.3.

Fig. 3.13 shows an open-drain bus circuit. The bus is a wire connected to pullup resistor R_{pu}. Each module on the bus has a pulldown transistor M_1, M_2, etc. If any of the devices turns on its pulldown transistor, the bus voltage is pulled to a low voltage. If no modules are on, the bus is kept at a high voltage thanks to the pullup resistor. If two modules turn on their pulldown transistors, the bus continues to operate normally. Open-collector and open-drain busses are robust because they are insensitive to multiple devices writing on the bus. However, the pullup transistor causes the bus to be relatively slow.

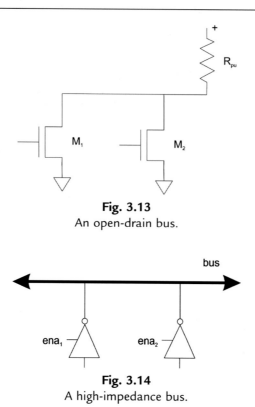

Fig. 3.13
An open-drain bus.

Fig. 3.14
A high-impedance bus.

Fig. 3.14 shows a high-impedance bus. Consider first a bus that is only a wire without a pullup resistor. Each module uses a three-state gate to connect to the bus. (We use inverting gates here but the polarity of the bus logic is not important to its circuit characteristics.) If one three-state gate is enabled, it controls the value on the bus. If two three-state gates are enabled and they output the same value, the bus continues to operate. If the two gates have opposite values, they will fight each other, resulting in at least a bad logic value on the bus and perhaps damage to the circuits. If no three-state gate is enabled, the bus is floating and does not have a reliable digital value. We can use a weak pullup to keep the bus at a valid logic value; the pullup is chosen to provide a small enough current that if a three-state gate can overcome it and determine the bus value.

3.6 Registers

We use the term **register** for any type of circuit used to locally store a bit value.

The simplest type of register is the SR latch, shown in Fig. 3.15. This latch does not have a clock input. Instead, its internal value is determined by the values of the set (S) and reset (R) inputs. SR latches are not widely used today because they may not reliably capture the intended value.

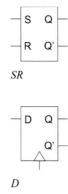

Fig. 3.15
Schematic symbols for SR and D registers.

SR latches made by hand from a pair of NOR or NAND gates are particularly unreliable—the parasitics of wiring affect the behavior of the latch too much.

Clocked registers are more reliable: a clock input determines when the data input value is read. The D register, also shown in Fig. 3.15, is one form of this type of register; other options also exist. Two major variants on the relationship between the clock and the internal state exist. A **level-sensitive** register, which we refer to as a latch, reads the data input into the register state so long as the clock signal is enabled. Once the clock signal is disabled, the internal state conforms to the last state on the data input. We call this form of register **transparent**. An **edge-triggered** register, which we refer to as a **flip-flop**, loads the register value only in a narrow interval around a clock edge.

Both types of registers must obey two timing constraints **setup** and **hold times**. Fig. 3.16 shows these timing requirements for the case of a positive edge-triggered registered. The setup time t_s

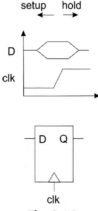

Fig. 3.16
Setup and hold times.

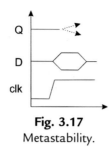

Fig. 3.17
Metastability.

is the time before the clock edge during which the data input must be stable. The hold time t_h is the time after the clock edge during which the data input must remain stable. In the case of a level-sensitive register, these times would be measured relative to the end of the active clock. If the data signal does not obey the setup and hold times, the register may store the wrong value. These times are often quoted as a combined setup-and-hold time.

A register's performance is given by its propagation delay from input to output: t_{PLH} for low-to-high transitions and t_{PHL} for high-to-low transitions.

Setup-and-hold time is an important design constraint because all registers can suffer from **metastability**. If the data value changes around the clock event, then the register may store an intermediate X state. As shown in Fig. 3.17, the register will eventually settle to a valid logic value but the time to do so is random and can be extremely long. When it does settle, it may settle on the wrong value. This phenomenon is often compared to a ball poised at the top of a hill; it may sit at the top for quite some time before a random wind blows it to one side of the hill or the other. We cannot eliminate metastability, we can only minimize it. Metastability is a particular concern when a register connects two regions that operate on different clocks—in this situation, some fraction of the inputs will inevitably fall in the metastability danger window.

We compute the probability of a metastable output based on a settling time S. The register has a time constant τ and setup/hold time t_{SH}. We also need to know the clock period. The probability of a metastable output failure at the end of the settling time is

$$P_F = \frac{t_{SH}}{T} e^{-S/\tau}. \tag{3.3}$$

The double-register structure of Fig. 3.18 is often used to minimize the effect of metastability. The logic must be designed to take into account the extra clock cycle of delay. The two levels of

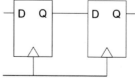

Fig. 3.18
Reducing metastability with a double-register.

register give the signal extra time to settle. The signal may settle to the wrong value, and there is still a chance that the second register may end up with an X. Occasionally, three levels of register are used to further reduce the chance of saving a metastable value.

3.7 Programmable Logic

We often need to design **glue logic** to perform basic operations in the interface. While small-scale integrated (SSI) circuits may be useful in some situations, chips that can implement more logic are often useful. **Complex programmable logic devices** (**CPLDs**).

A **field-programmable gate array** (**FPGA**) can implement multilevel logic—logical functions of varying depth. The two basic elements in an FPGA are programmable logic and programmable interconnect. A **programmable logic element** can be configured to represent a given logical function; typically an element has a limit on the number of inputs it can handle but can compute any logical function within that range of inputs. Programmable logic elements also include registers to store values. **Programmable interconnect** can be configured to make connections from the output of one logical element to the input of another. The most common means of configuring an FPGA uses static RAM (SRAM). Since SRAM loses its values when the power supply is removed, the FPGA must be configured whenever it is powered up. A **configuration file** is loaded into the FPGA to set the configuration of the logic elements and interconnect; specialized memories can be used to automatically load the configuration into the FPGA. We often refer to the configuration process as *programming* but this process is very different from programming a computer—an FPGA does not fetch and execute instructions.

We create a configuration file using **computer-aided design** (**CAD**) tools and **hardware description languages** (**HDLs**). Fig. 3.19 shows a simple HDL description in the Verilog

```
always @(posedge clk_samp)
begin
  if (rst_clk_samp)
  begin
    speed_cnt     <= 16'h0000;
  end
  else
  begin
    if (speed_cnt != 16'h0000)
    begin
      speed_cnt <= speed_cnt - 1'b1;
    end
    else begin
      speed_cnt <= SPEED_DIV;
    end
  end // if rst_clk_samp
end // always
```

Fig. 3.19
A simple Verilog description.

language; VHDL is the other major hardware description language. CAD tools first optimize the logic design, then determine where to place functions into logic elements and how to route elements between the logic elements. The result is a configuration file.

Programmable logic demands programmable I/O pins. FPGA and CPLD pins can be configured as input, output, or high impedance. Other aspects of the pin may also be configured. A common example is slew rate—the speed at which the output changes from 0 to 1 or 1 to 0. Fast signals demand high slew rates but signals that do not need to be fast can use a slow rate to reduce power consumption and electromagnetic interference.

Many advanced FPGAs are organized as a **system-on-chip** (**SoC**). In addition to a fabric of programmable logic elements and interconnect, they provide embedded memory, multipliers, one or several CPUs, and specialized I/O subsystems such as Ethernet.

3.8 CPU Interface Structures

CPUs may provide any of several different types of logic structures as interfaces to the CPU itself.

General-purpose I/O (**GPIO**) is a set of pins that are uncommitted to a particular purpose. GPIO pins can usually be configured to be either an input or an output.

Some microprocessors expose a bus to system designers, either their main bus or a bus specifically designed for I/O. The bus operates a **protocol** that determines what actions are taken by each device on the bus. The bus has a **master** that initiates operations. By default, the CPU is the master. The bus may provide a bus request signal to allow another device to temporarily become bus master.

Busses require different devices to drive some signals at different times—the CPU and memory, for example, may each write data onto the bus at different times. High-impedance or common drain/emitter circuits are often used at bus interfaces.

A simple example is shown in Fig. 3.20, which gives a timing diagram for a bus read operation. (Read/write directions are relative to the CPU when describing CPU busses.) The bus master presents an address on *adrs* and asserts *address ena*; the signals are timed to be valid before the rising *clk* edge. When the device is ready, it asserts *data* and *data ready*. In this simple protocol, the data is asserted for one clock cycle; some protocols may use a signal for the CPU to assert when it has captured the data.

Fig. 3.21 shows a logic schematic that provides the device's responsibilities for this protocol. The interface is designed to wait for the data to arrive from the interior of the device as signaled by *avail*. The *cmp* block compares the *adrs* value to the device's value. A protocol FSM controls the operation of the bus-side logic.

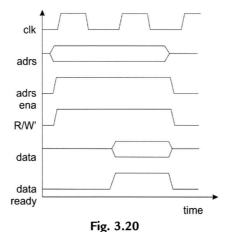

Fig. 3.20
Timing diagram for a bus read operation.

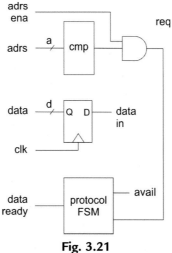

Fig. 3.21
Schematic for bus read logic.

Fig. 3.22 shows the state transition diagram for the protocol FSM. When *req* is asserted, the FSM waits for a data input from the remainder of the device. When that data is ready, the machine asserts *data ready* for one clock cycle to signal the bus master.

3.9 Logic Protection and Noise

Logic requires two types of protection from the outside world and from itself: **static electricity** and **electromagnetic interference (EMI)**.

CMOS logic is particularly sensitive to static electrical discharge. The gate oxide of a MOSFET is necessarily thin. Large voltages from static discharge can breakdown the MOSFET,

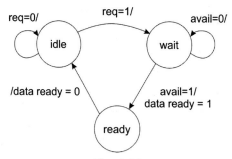

Fig. 3.22
State transition diagram for bus read protocol FSM.

rendering the circuit inoperative. When working on circuits, we should connect ourselves to ground using a **ground strap**.

The electrical signals on any wire generate electromagnetic fields. Wires also act as antennas that can receive the electromagnetic signals around them. We need to take steps to minimize both the EMI generated by circuits and the effect of EMI on our circuits. Reducing the slew rate of signals is an example of an active method of EMI minimization. Shielding—putting circuits in a metal box—both prevents generated EMI from being transmitted to the environment and protecting the circuits from external sources of EMI. We will discuss noise in more detail in Section 4.10.

Power supplies are an important source of noise for digital circuits. We have seen that our circuit models for logic gates depend on power supply voltages. Violating the power supply requirements will inevitably cause problems. We can reduce power supply noise, often called **power supply ripple**, using **decoupling capacitors** that is placed between the V_{DD} and V_{SS} power supply connections. Each decoupling capacitor serves a particular set of logic. As shown in Fig. 3.23, we may place decoupling capacitors at several points in the circuit. In many cases, we add a separate decoupling capacitor at each significant integrated circuit. The decoupling capacitor acts as a low-pass filter on the power supply; we can also view it as a charge reservoir for short-term use when the logic's current draw becomes too high for the power supply. Given logic current for n gates of nI_{max} and a maximum power supply ripple of $\triangle V$ over an interval t_{max}, the required decoupling capacitance is [74]:

$$C_D = nI_{max} \frac{t_{max}}{\triangle V} \tag{3.4}$$

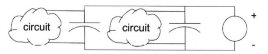

Fig. 3.23
Decoupling capacitors.

3.10 Auxiliary Devices and Circuits

The **light-emitting diode** (**LED**) is a common and very useful output device. Not only is an LED a useful indicator for the end user, but it can also be used during debugging to indicate signal state. Wiring an LED to a logic signal is straightforward but requires a little care. As shown in Fig. 3.24, the LED is connected in series with a resistor. The LED's orientation allows current to flow from the positive supply to ground. We can control the LED with the logic signal by using the logic signal as the positive terminal for the LED/resistor assembly. The current supplied by the driving logic gate determines the brightness of the LED. The resistor's role is to regulate current and provide a voltage drop. The LED's voltage is 0.7 V when it is on. The remaining voltage drop between the power supply terminals occurs over the resistor. We choose the value for the resistor based on the desired voltage drop and the current available from the driving gate:

$$V_R = V_{DD} - 0.7\,\text{V} \tag{3.5}$$

$$R = \frac{I_{out}}{V_R}. \tag{3.6}$$

Unless we need a particularly bright LED, we probably want to use a value for I_{out} lower than the data sheet maximum in order to avoid overstressing the driving gate.

The **optoisolator** combines an LED and a photosensitive transistor (in this case, a bipolar transistor) to create a logical signal path with no direct electrical connection. Fig. 3.25 shows the schematic symbol for an optoisolator. The output transistor's base acts as an optical detector; light from the input LED determines the output transistor's emitter-collector current. Optoisolators can be used to provide separate power supply circuits for different parts of the circuit, isolating one from the noise in the other circuit. As we will see in Section 3.11, we can use an optoisolator as a detector.

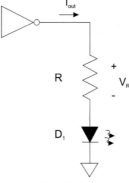

Fig. 3.24
An LED circuit.

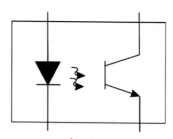

Fig. 3.25
Schematic symbol for an optoisolator.

Switches are often used for input. We have to take the mechanical characteristics of the switch into account within the interface. When a switch is closed—the contacts are pushed together to make a connection—the metal contacts bounce several times. As shown in Fig. 3.26, the switch will open and close many times in a short interval before it settles to its stable, closed value. We do not want to send all these events as a string of 1s and 0s to the CPU. Instead, we want to **debounce** the switch—temporarily force it to a single value until it settles. Of course, we want the user to be able to open the switch and turn off the connection. Given the short time scale of switch bouncing, the user does not observe any delay in being able to reopen the switch. We can any of several techniques to debounce a switch. We can do so in software using a CPU timer. At the other end of the spectrum, we can use the circuit in Fig. 3.27. When switch S_1 is open, R_1 charges C_1, providing a stable value logic 1 on the output. When the switch is closed, C_1 is drained through R_2, bringing the output voltage to a low level. We can easily manage the sense of the switch (logic 1 means open switch) in software.

A third option is a debouncer based on an integrated circuit known as a **one-shot**. The one-shot, also known as a *monostable multivibrator*, responds to a transition on its input by setting its output high for a given amount of time. At the end of the pulse, the one-shot's output returns to its original state. The length of the pulse is determined by a capacitor. By ORing (or NORing) together the raw switch signal with the one-shot pulse, we can smooth over the switch bounces. We will discuss one-shots in more detail in Section 5.10.

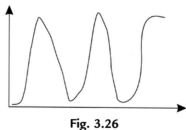

Fig. 3.26
Bouncing in a switch.

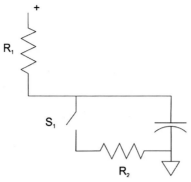

Fig. 3.27
A simple debouncing circuit.

Fig. 3.28
Schematic symbol for a Hall effect sensor.

A **Hall effect sensor** uses the interaction of magnetic fields and electric currents to detect the position of a magnet. Fig. 3.28 shows the schematic symbol for a Hall effect sensor. S magnetic field H imposes a force on an electric current I. The force causes the current t deflected, changing the voltage across the sensor. The Hall effect produces a linear variation in voltage from the magnetic field which we can use either for fine position of a magnet or as a nonlinear detector. For example, Hall effect sensors are commonly used to detect whether car doors are open or closed: a permanent magnet is placed on the door and the sensor body is placed in the door frame. The sensor reading indicates whether the magnet is next to the sensor—the door is closed—or whether the magnet is away from the sensor—the door is open. Hall effect sensors are also used in brushless DC motors to detect the position of the motor shaft.

3.11 Example: Shaft Encoder

We often need to detect the movement of a shaft: knobs on equipment turn shafts that are intended to control the equipment's operation; the position of a servo motor needs to be determined as an input to control. The **optical shaft encoder** is widely used thanks to its superior characteristics compared to mechanical or electromechanical alternatives: it provides low noise and low friction at a low cost.

Fig. 3.29
A simple shaft encoder mechanism.

Fig. 3.29 shows a simple shaft encoder. The shaft, made in this case from a paperclip, is fitted with a target of alternating white and black areas. That target is positioned in the middle of a variation of an optoisolator known as an **optical detector** or a **reflective optical switch**. This device points its LED output outward and provides a lens to capture reflected light. The target modulates the light that is reflected from the LED to the photodetector. The white and black areas of the target reflect different amounts of light depending on the position of the shaft. The output of the photodetector produces a signal that indicates when the target has been rotated from one area to the next. Optical detectors come in several configurations of the emitter and detector: parallel to each other, pointed at each other, and in this case reflected at an angle. These different arrangements are suited to different physical environments.

Fig. 3.30 shows a simple pattern for the target. The alternating black and white regions allow the detector to determine when the shaft has moved from one region to another; we can increase the resolution of the encoder by dividing the target into narrower slices. However, this target pattern gives us only a relative position for the shaft. The pattern of Fig. 3.31 encodes a three-bit position over the radius of the target (the white spacers between the target patterns were inserted for clarity and are not strictly necessary). We can use three optical detectors to read the three bits of the position. Those bits give us enough information to

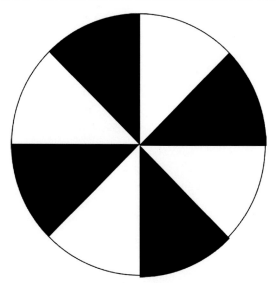

Fig. 3.30
A simple shaft encoder pattern.

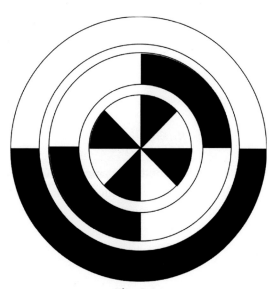

Fig. 3.31
An absolute position shaft encoder pattern.

determine which direction the shaft has turned and its absolute position to within 45 degrees. More tracks to the pattern and more detectors allow us to measure position more precisely. We can also add a separate track with a fiducial mark at a fixed position to provide a reference. This target uses a standard binary up-down code; a Gray code provides protection against mis-reads and glitches.

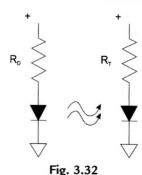

Fig. 3.32
Schematic for an optical detector circuit.

Our setup uses the OPB703WZ detector [72]. Fig. 3.32 shows the schematic for the detector circuits with the colors of the leads from the detectors as shown. We need to choose the values of the two resistors: R_D determines the amount of light produced by the LED; R_T determines the output current of the photodetector for a given amount of light. If the LED produces too much light for the photodetector, the detector's output will always be on; if the LED produces too little light for the photodetector, the detector will always be off. The two resistor values are related: the ratio R_D/R_T determines the relationship between LED output and photodetector sensitivity. The data sheet gives us some guidance to the proper resistor values.

- The LED forward DC current is $I_D = 40$ mA at a forward voltage of $V_D = 1.7$ V.
- The phototransistor collector DC current is 3.5 mA at an emitter-collector voltage of 5 V.

Once we choose the power supply voltage, we can find

$$R_D = \frac{V_{DD} - V_D}{I_D}. \tag{3.7}$$

On the output side, we need to check two conditions: the logic 0 output value produced by the photodetector is compatible with the next stage of logic; and that the on current produced by the photodetector is sufficient to drive the next stage.

Further Reading

Wakerly [73] provides a thorough introduction to logic design.

Questions

Q3.1   A CMOS gate has a maximum current of 4 mA at a power supply voltage of 5 V. Given an LED on voltage of 0.7 V, what value of resistor should be used if we want to draw half the maximum allowable current to light the LED?

Q3.2   An LED is driven by an inverter to display a logic value. The inverter can supply a maximum output current of 2.5 mA. The power supply voltage is 3.3 V. What value of resistor should be used to draw an on current of half the inverter's maximum rating?

Q3.3   An LED is driven by a series 5 kΩ resistor. Given a power supply voltage of 3.3 V, what is the diode current?

Q3.4   What conditions govern the value of a pullup resistor for an open-drain connection?

Q3.5   A CMOS gate operates at $V_{CC} = 3.3$ V, $V_{IH} = 3.15$ V, $V_{IL} = 1.35$ V. How much drive current must the gate provide on a $1 \rightarrow 0$ transition to a gate with input capacitance of 15 pF to achieve a delay of 10 ns?

Q3.6   A CMOS gate rising input follows an exponential curve with time constant $\tau = 3$ ns. The gate operates on a power supply of 3.3 V. If the logic levels are $V_{IH} = 3.15$ V, $V_{IL} = 1.35$ V, how long is the gate input in the unknown region?

Q3.7   A CMOS logic family has an input capacitance of 15 pF and an output current of 20 mA. It operates at a power supply voltage of 3.3 V. What is the maximum fanout to ensure transition times less than 15 ns?

Q3.8   Draw a timing diagram for the operation of a D register. The timing diagram should include a setup time of 20 ns and hold time of 7 ns.

Q3.9   A register has a time constant of $\tau = 3$ ns, a setup/hold time of $t_{SH} = 27$ ns. Its input clock has a period of 50 ns. How long must it be given to settle to ensure a metastability probability below 10^{-20}?

Q3.10   A CMOS logic family draws current of 10 mA at a power supply voltage of 3 V. You are given a block of logic with 20 gates. How much decoupling capacitance is required to ensure a maximum power supply drop of 10% over 5 ns?

Q3.11   Design a modified form of the bus interface of Section 3.8 that allows for variable timing of the register read.

       (a)   Modify the timing diagram to use a *data ack* signal to acknowledge the read by the CPU.

       (b)   Draw a state transition diagram for the FSM.

CHAPTER 4

Amplifiers

4.1 Introduction

Amplifiers represent the simplest transformation we make on signals—we turn a small signal into a larger, more powerful version of the same. But this simple task involves many subtleties. Mastering amplification is useful in itself as well as an important exercise in circuit design.

Designing amplifiers requires us to understand transistors in more detail. Discrete transistors can be used to build a wide range of amplifiers. Fig. 4.1 shows two types of packages: TO-220

Fig. 4.1
Two types of transistor packages.

Embedded System Interfacing. https://doi.org/10.1016/B978-0-12-817402-9.00004-2
65

on the left and TO-92 on the right. We will also study integrated amplifiers in the form of op amps.

The next section introduces the basic specifications for amplifiers. Section 4.3 discusses analysis methods for circuits. Section 4.4 develops circuit models for the MOSFET. Section 4.5 introduces amplifier topologies. Section 4.6 designs an amplifier for a low-impedance load. Section 4.7 briefly introduces concepts in power amplifiers. Section 4.8 considers integrated amplifiers as useful components. Section 4.9 introduces the op amp, a versatile component. Section 4.10 considers noise, interference, and crosstalk. Section 4.11 looks at the design of an amplifier for a microphone.

4.2 Amplifier Specifications

We use amplifiers because they provide **gain**, represented by the variable A. We can talk about power, voltage, or current gain, depending on how we prefer to think about the signals. The most common form used in amplifier design is voltage gain:

$$A_V = \frac{V_{out}}{V_{in}}. \tag{4.1}$$

A negative value for gain means that the output is 180 degrees out of phase with the input: when the input is high, the output is low; when the input is low, the output is high. Many amplifier topologies naturally produce inverted outputs and are characterized by negative gain.

We are particularly concerned with the load impedance that the amplifier is able to drive. The input characteristics of the amplifier are also of interest.

Since neither the devices nor circuits that make up the amplifier are ideal, we are also interested in specifying the tolerable level of variations from the ideal. When we compare the output of an amplifier to a known input, such as a sinusoid, we measure its **distortion**. Some forms of distortion are linear; they generate **harmonic distortion**. When we inject a sinusoidal signal P_F at the **fundamental frequency** into the amplifier's input, harmonic distortion appears as a set of harmonic signals $P_{H,\,i}$. We can define **total harmonic distortion (THD)** as

$$THD = \frac{\sum_i P_{H,i}}{P_F}. \tag{4.2}$$

Nonharmonic distortions are known as **intermodulation distortion (IM)**. When we inject two sinusoids that are not harmonically related into the amplifier's input, intermodulation generates signals at other frequencies. If the input signals are at frequencies $f_1, f_2, f_2 > f_1$, the intermodulation products include sums and products of multiples of the input frequencies:

$$mf_1 + nf_2, n, m = 1, 2, \ldots. \tag{4.3}$$

The *order* of the harmonic is given by $m+n$. Intermodulation products that are near the frequency of interest are of particular concern. We generally measure the different intermodulation products individually and measure the ratio of the RMS intermodulation voltage to the fundamental RMS voltage.

Another important form of nonideality is **noise**. We specify amplifiers based on **signal-to-noise ratio** (**SNR**), or the ratio between the largest signal the amplifier can produce to the noise it produces; we also refer to this ratio as **dynamic range.** These values are often cited in decibels. We will discuss noise, interference, and crosstalk in Section 4.10.

4.3 Circuit Analysis Methods

Transistors are nonlinear, active elements that we can use to build linear circuits. Amplifiers are very useful in themselves; amplifier design also allows us to learn and practice a wide range of circuit analysis and design techniques.

Circuit designers often refer to **DC** and **AC analysis**. Since we can break down any signal into the sum of a constant value and a changing value, we can use this decomposition to help us understand circuits. DC analysis assumes no signals in the circuit change. We often want to place some terminals of a transistor at a given voltage known as a **bias voltage**. The device may require that some terminals are kept at a prescribed voltage: bipolar transistors require a voltage across their base-emitter junction to turn on the transistor; MOSFETs require their gate voltage to be above the threshold voltage. We may also want to put some terminals at a given voltage to ensure that signals, when they do change, can swing through their full range. DC analysis allows us to determine bias voltages and the **operating point** of the transistor. AC analysis can separately consider the effects of changing signals. We traditionally use capital letters for DC variables (I_1, V_1) and lowercase letters for AC variables (i_2, v_2).

Circuit designers also refer to **small-signal** and **large-signal analysis**. While transistors are nonlinear devices, we can approximate them with linear models over some of their operating range and under the assumption that signals are small. A **small-signal model** provides an equivalent circuit for a transistor under conditions that allow the transistor to be treated as a linear component. Under small-signal analysis, we replace the device with its small-signal model; we also replace DC voltage sources with short circuits and DC current sources with open circuits. We typically use small letters such as i_1, v_1 for small-signal values. However, small-signal assumptions do not hold in some circuits, with power amplifiers being a classic example. We use **large-signal models** in these cases. Typically, we use graphical methods to solve for the behavior of the transistor under large-signal assumptions: starting with the set of operating curves for the transistor, we draw additional lines that represent the constraints imposed on the transistor operation by other circuit components.

We will take advantage of schematic capture and simulation tools in this chapter. Circuit simulators, as described in Section 1.9, allow us to solve for the waveforms of complex circuits with nonlinear elements; they also provide other forms of analysis such as noise. Free versions of CAD tools are limited in capability relative to paid tools but still provide valuable capabilities.

4.4 MOSFET Transistor Models

We can model the MOSFET using both small-signal and large-signal models. For each model, we need to determine the model parameters from the given parameters of the particular transistor we want to use. Data sheets may or may not directly give us the required parameters; in such cases we need to derive the model parameters from the given values.

We will use as an example the Fairchild BS170 n-type MOSFET [18]. Fig. 4.2 gives some of this transistor's parameters.

4.4.1 Small-Signal Models

Figs. 4.3 and 4.4 show two small-signal models for a MOSFET: the **pi model** takes the form of the Greek letter; the **t model** uses a T-shaped circuit topology. These two models are equivalent; in any given situation, one may be more convenient than the other. The diamond-shaped current source represents a **controlled source**—the current depends on another circuit variable.

The transistor's **transconductance** g_m relates input voltage to output current. The MOSFET gate's high capacitance gives an open circuit in this model. The resistance r_0 models the resistance between the drain and source. In the t model form, the gate current is always zero.

Threshold voltage V_T	2.1V
Drain-source on resistance R_{ds}	1.2Ω
Transconductance g_m	320 mA/V
Gate capacitance C_g	24 pF
Maximum drain-source voltage	60V
Maximum continuous current	500 mA

Fig. 4.2
Characteristics of the BS170 n-type MOSFET.

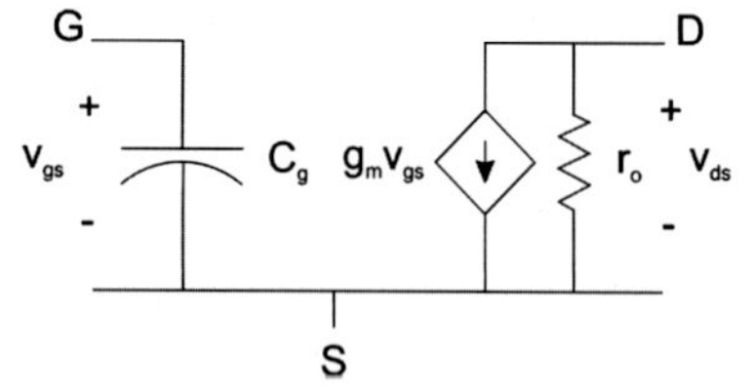

Fig. 4.3
A small-signal pi model for a MOSFET.

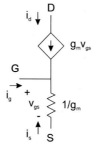

Fig. 4.4
A small-signal t model for a MOSFET.

4.4.2 Large-Signal Models

As we saw in Section 3.3, a MOSFET has a **linear region** corresponding to low drain-source voltages and a **saturation region** corresponding to high V_{DS}. It also has a **cutoff region** when the gate voltage is below the device's threshold voltage, but that is not directly represented in the characteristic curves.

$$\text{Cutoff}: I_D = 0, V_{GS} < V_t. \tag{4.4}$$

$$\text{Linear}: I_D = k'\frac{W}{L}\left[(V_{GS}-V_t)V_{DS}-V_{DS}^2\right], V_{DS} < V_{GS} - V_t. \tag{4.5}$$

$$\text{Saturation}: I_D = \frac{1}{2}k'\frac{W}{L}(V_{GS}-V_t)^2, V_{DS} \geq V_{GS} - V_t. \tag{4.6}$$

The large-signal model [57] reflects these three modes of operation. Fig. 4.5 shows a simple large-signal model for a MOSFET's saturation mode. The voltage across the gate capacitance controls the drain-source current source.

V_t is the **threshold voltage** below which the MOSFET drain-source region does not conduct. k' is a parameter that depends on device physics. W/L gives the width/length ratio of the MOSFET channel, which scales the magnitude of the current; this parameter is of more interest

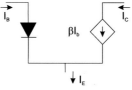

Fig. 4.5
A large-signal model for saturation mode operation of a MOSFET.

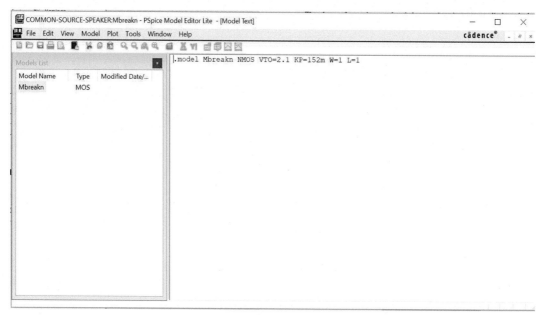

Fig. 4.6
PSpice model for the BS170 n-type MOSFET.

to integrated circuit designers who can choose the sizes of their transistors. When using discrete MOSFETs we are generally given the drain current for a given gate voltage.

To properly simulate this transistor in PSpice, we need to set the MOSFET model parameter using the Model Editor shown in Fig. 4.6. The PSpice model was designed for integrated circuit design in which we know the width and length of the transistor channel. In this case, we set the transistor width and length to 1. We estimate $k' = {2I_{D,max}} \big/ \left(V_{DS,max} - V_t\right) = 152\,\text{mS}$.

We can trace the characteristic curves of a MOSFET. Fig. 4.7 shows the setup. In this case, the gate is driven by a voltage source. We sweep both the drain-source voltage and the gate voltage. The results are shown in Fig. 4.8. These curves clearly show the linear and saturation regions of the transistor's operation.

4.5 MOSFET Amplifier Topologies

We can incorporate the MOSFET into amplifiers with several different topologies. Each has its own advantages and disadvantages.

4.5.1 Common Source Amplifier

Fig. 4.9 shows a **common source** amplifier. This topology provides good voltage gain. The high gate impedance of the MOSFET gives this topology a high input impedance.

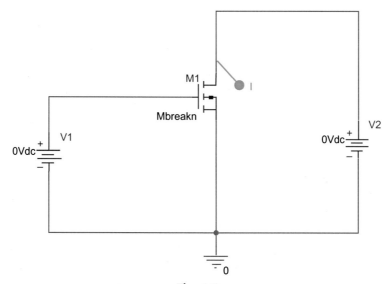

Fig. 4.7
A curve tracer circuit for a MOSFET.

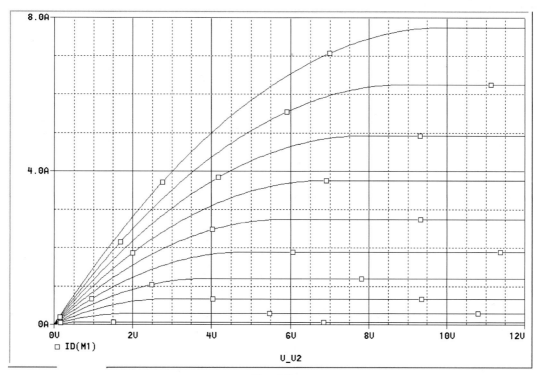

Fig. 4.8
A simulated curve tracing of a MOSFET.

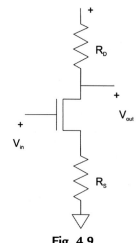

Fig. 4.9
A common source amplifier.

We can analyze the voltage gain of the common source amplifier using AC analysis and the MOSFET small-signal model of Fig. 4.10. The input source and power supply become shorts in AC analysis. The model circuit is shown in Fig. 4.10. If $r_0 \gg R_D$, the output voltage is $V_{ds} = g_m V_{gs} R_D$; the input voltage is $V_{gs} = (g_m + 1) V_{gs} R_S$. When we substitute these terms into the definition of voltage gain, we find

$$A_v = \frac{g_m V_{gs} R_D}{(g_m + 1) V_{gs} R_S} \approx \frac{R_D}{R_S}. \tag{4.7}$$

Large-signal analysis starts with a **load line** for the circuit—the load line describes the drain-source current over a range of drain-source voltages. Fig. 4.11 shows that in this case the load

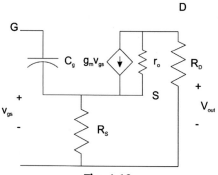

Fig. 4.10
A small-signal model for common source amplifier gain.

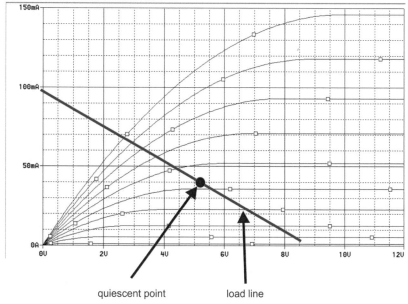

Fig. 4.11
A load line plot for an amplifier.

line is defined by V_{DD} on one end and V_{DD}/R_L at the other end. We select a **quiescent point** or **Q point** that represents V_{DS} when the input is zero; the Q point is typically put at the middle of the operating region of the load line.

4.5.2 Common Drain Amplifier

Fig. 4.12 shows the **common drain** or **source follower** configuration. This topology provides unity voltage gain and a relatively high output impedance that makes it useful for driving low-impedance loads. Once again, the MOSFET's gate impedance ensures high input impedance.

4.5.3 Common Gate Amplifier

Fig. 4.13 shows **the common gate** configuration. This configuration provides unity current gain and good voltage gain. Because the gate is not at the input, it has low input impedance. It provides a high output impedance making it useful for driving low-impedance loads.

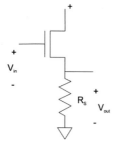

Fig. 4.12
A common drain or source follower amplifier.

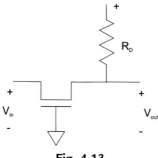

Fig. 4.13
A common gate amplifier.

4.5.4 Cascode Amplifier

We can also design a cascode amplifier using MOSFETs as shown in Fig. 4.14. M_1 is configured as a common emitter while M_2 is used as an emitter follower. The signal input is provided to the gate of M_2.

4.5.5 Differential Amplifier

Fig. 4.15 shows the differential amplifier. This topology is widely used to compare two signals and amplify the difference between them. The currents of the two legs defined by M_1, M_2 are related to each other through the current source—the sum of the currents through the two legs is constant. Differences in the input voltages V_+, V_- result in amplified differences in the output voltages V_1, V_2.

4.5.6 Current Sources

The differential amplifier makes use of a current source as do many other circuits. An ideal current source produces a known current independent of load. We can build realistic current sources with various degrees of fidelity to that goal, each with its own advantages and disadvantages.

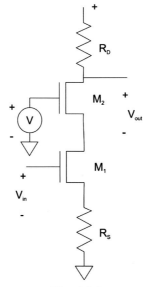

Fig. 4.14
A MOSFET cascode amplifier.

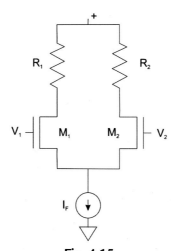

Fig. 4.15
A MOSFET differential amplifier.

Fig. 4.16 shows a basic current source circuit. The voltage divider provides a gate voltage for the MOSFET that governs its drain-source current. This circuit is adequate for simple applications but is prone to several problems: variations in the power supply voltage will cause variations in the output current; temperature variations will cause the transistor gain to change, resulting in a change in the output current; inaccuracies in the resistor values will cause an unanticipated output current.

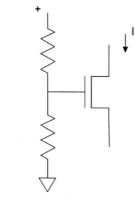

Fig. 4.16
A simple current source.

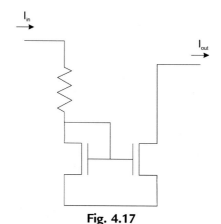

Fig. 4.17
A Widlar current mirror.

A **current mirror** is used to copy an input current to an output current while isolating the input from the output. Current mirrors are designed with low input impedance to minimize input voltage variations; they provide high output impedance to reduce variations caused by the load. Several current mirror circuits have been designed; one example is the Widlar current mirror of Fig. 4.17. Accurate current mirrors require matched transistors so building one out of discrete transistors may be counterproductive. Several integrated circuit current mirrors are available that take advantage of the good matching characteristics of ICs.

4.6 Example: Driving a Low-Impedance Load

We can use the basic amplifier circuits to build a two-stage amplifier designed to drive a low-impedance load using MOSFETs. Given a circuit topology for the amplifier, we can derive several models for different analytical purposes. For each stage, we establish some large-signal parameters and then use those values to determine the component values.

This example gives us the chance to consider some practicalities. While we may calculate particular values for our components, we can't procure components with those exact values. Resistors, inductors, and capacitors all come in standard values. Those values are chosen to provide a good range of values and avoid gaps in coverage. Nonetheless, we must make use of the available values, which is one reason to design robust circuits that are tolerant of variations.

Beyond choosing fixed values, we must take into account the fact that passive components are manufactured to certain **tolerances**. For example, a 47 kΩ resistor with a tolerance of $\pm10\%$ could have an actual value ranging from 42.3 to 5.17 $k\Omega$. Components are generally available in several different tolerances; tighter tolerances cost more money. **Matching** of component values is particularly important for symmetric circuits. For example, the difference in value of the two resistors on the legs of a differential amplifier has a greater effect on the performance of the amplifier than does their absolute values, at least within reasonable tolerances. Unmatched resistors in the two legs of the differential pair lead to different voltages and currents in the legs even when the input voltages are identical.

Passive components are also given maximum power ratings. A component should not be operated at a power level higher than its rating. In general, some amount of headroom should be left in the power rating. Given the variation of component values and other operating conditions, devices operating at close to their rated power level may occasionally exceed that level, causing reliability problems.

4.6.1 Amplifier Specifications and Topology

Fig. 4.18 shows the OrCAD schematic for the amplifier, which is organized into two stages. The first stage uses M_1 in a common-source configuration; the second stage uses M_2 as a source follower/common-drain.

The amplifier is designed around a 12 V power supply. Our specifications include a voltage gain $A_v = -10$ and the ability to drive an 8 Ω load, which is the typical impedance for a large speaker (smaller speakers generally have a 4 Ω impedance). The amplifier should work over the standard audio range of $[f_L, f_H] = [100 \text{ Hz}, 20 \text{ kHz}]$. We assume that the impedance of the source is 1 kΩ. We can choose the component values starting at the input and, for the most part, move through to the output. We will simulate the circuit using the transistor model we used in Section 4.4.1.

4.6.2 Input and First Stage

We will use the BS170 MOSFET for both stages [18]; it has a maximum voltage of 60 V and $g_m = 320$ mS, $k' = 17$ mS, $V_T = 2.1$ V, $I_{D,SAT} = 0.5$ A.

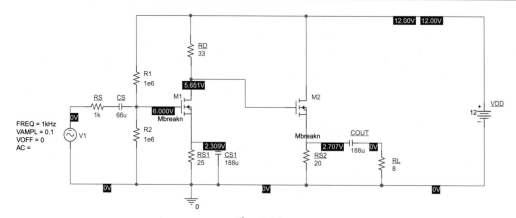

Fig. 4.18
A two-stage MOSFET amplifier.

The first stage will supply all of the voltage gain for the amplifier. Given that we use the second stage for current amplification, we have some freedom in how we choose the maximum drain current, so we choose a value of $I_{max}=0.4$ A which occurs at $V_{min}=2.3$ V. Fig. 4.19 shows the load line based on the transistor curves, the power supply voltage, and the chosen drain current. We choose $V_Q=7.25$ V as an quiescent point, the midpoint of the operating region of the load line.

We use the voltage gain and collector current to determine the values for R_D and R_{S1}. Within the desired frequency response of the amplifier, R_{S1} is shorted out by C_{S1}. We can determine the value for R_D by substituting the small-signal MOSFET model into a small-signal model of the amplifier. As shown in Fig. 4.20, the power supply appears as a short in the small-signal model, so R_D is connected in parallel with the MOSFET's internal resistance r_o. Since $R_D \gg r_o$, we can approximate the gain as

$$A_v = \frac{v_{ds}}{v_{gs}} \approx -g_m R_D. \tag{4.8}$$

Substituting our values for A_v and g_m, we find that $R_F=33$ Ω.

We choose R_{S1} to provide a reasonable voltage between the MOSFET's source and ground, one large enough to allow for the maximum output swing of the first stage. If we allow a maximum swing of $V_{1max}=5$ V at a current of $I_{D1max}=0.2$ A, then

$$R_{S1} = \frac{V_{1max}}{I_{D1max}} = 25 \, \Omega. \tag{4.9}$$

The resistors R_1 and R_2 are the bias network for M_1. They form a voltage divider to set the gate voltage for M_1: their ratio determines the bias voltage while their sum determines the current

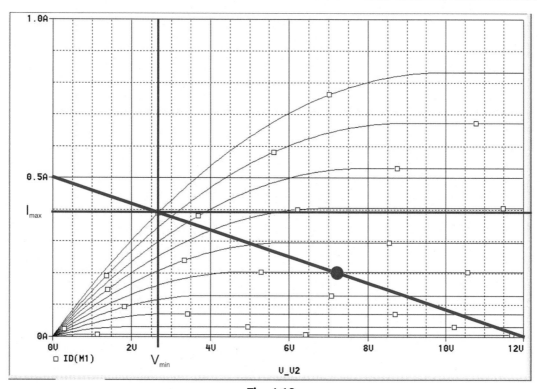

Fig. 4.19
Load line for the first stage of the two-stage amplifier.

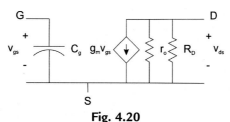

Fig. 4.20
Small-signal model for first stage gain.

running through the bias circuit. We have chosen a bias voltage for the gate of 6 V. Given the MOSFET's high impedance, we have a great deal of freedom in choosing the bias resistor values. A good approach is to choose large values that result in a small current in the bias network. We choose $R_1 = R_2 = 1\,\text{M}\Omega$.

We also need to find a value for the source bypass capacitor C_{S1}. The parallel combination of R_{S1}, C_{S1} should appear as a short within the operating frequency range of the amplifier. We achieve this by setting the -3 dB point of C_S, R_S should be at $f_L = 100$ Hz. We know from

Section 1.4 that the −3 dB point occurs at half power or $1/\sqrt{2}$ voltage. This condition occurs when the resistance equals the capacitive reactance:

$$C_{S1} = \frac{1}{2\pi f_{LS} R_{S1}}.$$

(4.10)

We also need to find a value for the input coupling capacitor C_S. This capacitor DC-decouples the input from the transistor's bias network. We substitute into Eq. (4.10) to find that $C_S = 63$ μF which we round to $C_S = 66$ μF.

Fig. 4.21 shows the output of the first stage. The measured gain is approximately 5, lower than the target value for the gain. The initial drift in voltage is due to the charging of the capacitors.

4.6.3 Second Stage and Output

The second stage does not need a bias network because the first stage output maintains a reasonable operating voltage for M_2. This stage uses a common drain topology, also known as a source follower, to provide strong drive to the low-impedance output without increasing voltage gain. This topology means that there is no drain resistor.

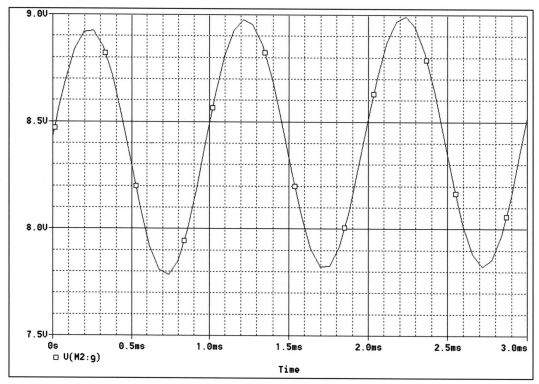

Fig. 4.21
Output of the first stage of the two-stage amplifier.

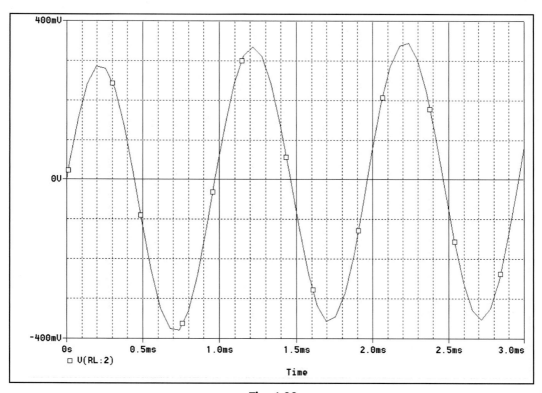

Fig. 4.22
Output of the second stage of the two-stage amplifier.

We choose the source resistance R_{S2} to ensure that the worst-case voltage swing does not push the MOSFET's source voltage to the negative power supply:

$$R_{S2} = \frac{V_{DD} - V_{min}}{I_{Dmax} - I_{Lmax}}. \tag{4.11}$$

We choose a minimum source voltage of $V_{min} = 3$ V and a maximum drain current of $I_{Dmax} = 0.5$ A. If we allow a maximum current to the load of $I_{Lmax} = 0.05$ A, then we find $R_{S2} = 20\ \Omega$ which we approximate as $R_{S2} = 25\ \Omega$.

We set the value of $C2$ to provide an appropriate rolloff frequency given the load resistance of $8\ \Omega$, giving us $C2 = 199\ \mu$F which we approximate as $C2 = 188\ \mu$F.

Fig. 4.22 shows output waveform for the amplifier's second stage as measured across R_L.

4.7 Power Amplifiers

The amplifier techniques from Section 4.6 are not always suited to the design of large power amplifiers. We do not often need to build our own power amplifiers for computer interfaces but a brief discussion helps to highlight some interesting aspects of amplifier design.

Linear amplifiers generate higher-powered output signals that follow their lower-powered inputs. By biasing the amplifier in different ways, we can create different **classes** of amplifier with different characteristics.

A **Class A** amplifier is biased to the middle of its operating range, allowing symmetric input signal swings. The amplifiers of Section 4.small-signal-amp were designed for Class A operation. Class A amplifiers offer the least distortion but also the highest power consumption. When the input voltage is zero, the Class A amplifier produces a large output current and consuming power.

A **Class B** amplifier is biased so that it operates for only half of the waveform. Since we often want to amplify both sides of the input waveform, we can connect two Class B drivers in a push-pull configuration. One driver pulls up for positive outputs while the other driver pulls down for negative outputs. The Class B amplifier stages do not produce output currents when the input voltage is zero. The tradeoff for lower power consumption is somewhat higher distortion. We can build Class AB amplifiers by biasing the drivers so that each operates for more than half of the input cycle, somewhat reducing distortion.

A **Class C** amplifier amplifies for less than half of the input cycle.

Class D amplifiers are not linear. The D does not stand for digital, however. These amplifiers use pulse width modulation to modulate the power supplied to the output [29]. An output filter transforms the pulse-modulated train into the desired continuous signal. Class D amplifiers are extremely power efficient; they can be operated without heat sinks up to a surprisingly high output power level. Class D amplifiers for speakers, which present inductive loads, share some design issues with motor controllers; we will discuss motor controllers in more detail in Section 8.13.

Thermal dissipation is an important design consideration for power amplifiers. Most of the electrical energy put into the circuit comes out as heat. If the components become too hot, they will degrade and eventually fail. While all components are subject to heat problems, transistors are most critical to protect. When the interior of the transistor reaches the **maximum junction temperature** $T_j = 85°C$, the semiconductor junctions of the device are damaged. We use **heat sinks** to help dissipate the heat energy generated by transistors.

We can calculate the junction temperature using a steady-state model. Each component has a **thermal resistance** which describes the flow of heat. The transistor data sheet provides a thermal resistance from junction to case; in the case of our example transistor, $R_{\theta JC} = 83.3°C/W$ [20]. The heat sink has its own thermal resistance $R_{\theta HS}$. For our simple model, we can consider these two thermal resistances to be in series, much as electrical resistances. Power dissipation in the heat equation is analogous to current in electrical circuits. The amplifier operates in an environment at an **ambient temperature**; the environment is analogous to ground in an electrical circuit. We can find the junction temperature as the increase in temperature above the ambient given the thermal resistance and power consumption:

$$T_J = T_A + P(R_{\theta JC} + R_{\theta HS}). \tag{4.12}$$

4.8 Integrated Amplifiers

As much fun as it is to design and build your own transistor amplifiers, using an integrated amplifier often makes more sense. Integrated circuits provide much better matching of components and lower parasitic values, improving amplifier performance. Integrated amplifiers are also physically small.

The TPA6138A2 [64] is designed to drive headphones, providing 40 mW into 32 Ω. External resistors are used to set the amplifier gain. It includes circuitry to reduce clicks and pops caused by plugging and unplugging the headphones.

The LM380 [40] is a 2.5 W power amplifier for audio. It provides a fixed gain of 50 (34 dB) to reduce the cost of the circuit; volume control can be provided by preamplifier stages feeding the LM380.

The TPA6404-Q1 [69] is designed for automotive audio systems. At its core is a 50 W class D amplifier. It provides control and diagnostics using the I^{2}C bus. Some amplifiers provide digital input. The TAS6424L-Q1 [68], for example, provides I^{2}C input of the audio channels as well as control and diagnostics.

The WM9801 [13] combines a DAC with an amplifier. The chip provides both class AB and class D amplifier modes. Digital logic is used for filtering, volume control, parametric equalization, and dynamic range control.

The LM386 [70] is a widely used low-voltage audio power amplifier. It can operate on power supply voltages in the range 4–12 V with gains in the range 20–200. Its low power supply voltage and reasonable gain make it popular in small guitar amplifiers and portable consumer audio equipment.

4.9 Op Amps

Integrated audio amplifiers are designed for particular applications. The **operational amplifier** or **op amp**, in contrast, is designed as a general-purpose component used to build specific circuits. Op amps are used in all sorts of ways in circuit design. We will cover more sophisticated uses of op amps in more detail in Chapter 5; here we concentrate on their use as amplifiers.

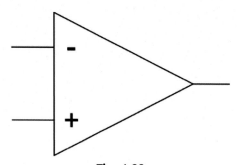

Fig. 4.23
Schematic symbol for an op amp.

The schematic symbol for an op amp is shown in Fig. 4.23. It has two inputs, + and −. The one output value is formed by the difference of the two inputs. An op amp requires a power source but we will typically omit their power connections in our illustrations. The 741 is a classic op amp but other designs provide a range of operating characteristics.

An ideal op amp has three basic characteristics:

• Infinite input impedance.
• Infinite gain.
• Zero output impedance.

Real op amps cannot provide these superlative characteristics but reasonable circuits can provide very good approximations of them over a wide range of frequencies. A typical op amp circuit is built from two major blocks: a differential amplifier compares the two input voltages; a voltage amplifier is used to provide voltage gain for the differential amplifier's result. Op amps are mainstays for small-signal amplification. While op amps generally do not provide the drive capability required for large power amplifiers, they can be used as an input stage. Many power amplifiers also use differential input stages similar to those used in op amps.

An op amp without feedback will produce output voltages at one extreme or the other based on the polarity of $V_+ - V_-$. We generally use feedback circuits to control the op amp.

Fig. 4.24 shows a linear amplifier built from an op amp [41]. This is an inverting amplifier with voltage gain

$$A_V = -\frac{R_2}{R_1}. \tag{4.13}$$

For example, $R_2 = 10$ kΩ, $R_1 = 1$ kΩ gives $A_V = 10$. This formula is easy to derive. Since the input terminals have infinite impedance, no current flows into them so:

$$\frac{V_{in}}{R_1} = -\frac{V_{out}}{R_2}. \tag{4.14}$$

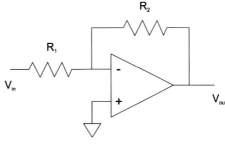

Fig. 4.24
An inverting linear amplifier based on an op amp.

We can rearrange the terms and obtain the gain formula of Eq. (4.13).

Fig. 4.25 shows a noninverting topology for an amplifier. The gain in this case is

$$A_v = \frac{R_1 + R_2}{R_1}. \tag{4.15}$$

In the noninverting case, $R_2 = 10$ kΩ, $R_1 = 1$ kΩ gives $A_V = 11$.

Fig. 4.26 shows an op amp used to generate the difference between the two inputs. When all four resistors have the same value, the output is $V_B - V_A$. We can generate weighted differences by changing the relative values of the resistors.

Real op amps have nonideal characteristics that will affect circuit design to some degree [32]. The most important is its finite bandwidth. We evaluate bandwidth using open loop gain. While an op amp has a very high (albeit finite) gain, that gain starts to roll off quickly: the -3 dB point of the μA741 op amp is about 5 Hz [60]; other op amps may roll off at hundreds of hertz. The gain rolls off at 6 *dB* per decade. The **unity gain point** is the frequency at which the op amp's gain is 1. The μA741, for example, has a unity gain frequency of about 1 MHz. When we use the

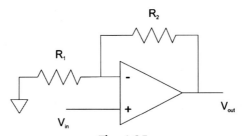

Fig. 4.25
A noninverting linear amplifier based on an op amp.

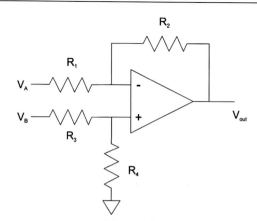

Fig. 4.26
An op amp difference amplifier.

op amp in a closed-loop circuit, we want to be sure that the closed loop gain at the maximum required frequency is considerably larger than the op amp's open loop gain at that frequency. A good rule of thumb is that the op amp should have an open loop bandwidth of at least $10X$ the required closed-loop bandwidth [32].

Slew rate describes the large-signal behavior of the op amp; slew rate is also used to evaluate other types of amplifiers. Slew rate is defined as the ratio of change in output voltage per unit time:

$$SR = \frac{\triangle V_{max}}{\triangle t}.$$
(4.16)

Slew rate is limited by the amplifier's maximum output current. The μA741 has a slew rate at unity gain of 0.5 V/μs.

The noise of an op amp will limit the dynamic range through which it can be operated.

Common mode rejection ratio (**CMRR**) measures the response of the op amp to the same voltage on both its input terminals. The magnitude of CMRR is equal to the inverse of the ratio of the common mode output voltage to the common mode input.

In any feedback circuit we need to be concerned about stability. Parasitics internal to the op amp can create undesired feedback that results in instability. In some cases, we may need to add compensation capacitors to ensure the stability of the op amp.

4.10 Noise, Interference, and Crosstalk

Noise in its most general sense refers to any unwanted signal. Noise can come from many different sources, including from the components we use to build our electronic systems.

Statistical models help us to understand noise. Physical systems exhibit noise that can be classified under several different models. **White noise** is uncorrelated from moment to moment; as a result, it has a flat power spectrum with equal levels of power at all frequencies. We often use a Gaussian distribution to model the amplitude of a white noise signal:

$$w(x) = \frac{1}{\sqrt{2\pi\sigma^2}} e^{-(x-\mu)^2/2\sigma^2},$$
(4.17)

where μ, σ are the mean and variance, respectively. **Shot noise** is generated by the discrete nature of electrons. This form of noise is modeled as a Poisson distribution. **1/f noise** or **pink noise** is widely observed in nature but its physical basis is poorly understood. As its name implies, its power spectral density is proportional to $1/f$.

Thermal noise is inherent in physical systems. In electronic systems, this form of noise in conductors is known as **Johnson noise** or **Johnson-Nyquist noise**. This form of noise depends on the resistance of the component and is defined as a power spectral density per hertz of bandwidth:

$$\overline{v_n^2} = 4kTR,$$
(4.18)

where k is Boltzmann's constant, T is temperature in Kelvin, and R is resistance in Ohms. Since this formulation results in an infinite noise power level over an unbounded bandwidth, we define the noise relative to the bandwidth of interest in the circuit.

We sometimes want to generate noise. As one example, music synthesizers use random noise as input to synthesizer functions to create more natural sounds. We can generate noise either using analog or digital methods. In the case of digital methods, we often use **pseudorandom** algorithms that are deterministic but create sequences of outputs that obey a desired distribution. A common approach is to first generate a uniformly distributed sequence and then shape the sequence to the desired distribution.

We will use the term **interference** to refer to an unwanted signal that comes from outside of our circuit of interest. Interference may come from another part of our circuit or from a completely outside source. Designers have to worry both about generating interference and dealing with interference from other devices. Depending on their application, some circuits may require certification by the Federal Communications Commission (FCC) or other regulatory bodies.

Radio frequency interference (**RFI**) results in both digital and analog circuits. The wires and electrical leads in electronic systems act as antennas that can both emit radio signals caused by the signals that flow through them and can pick up signals emitted by other electronic systems. We are particularly concerned with RFI at higher frequencies. The optimum length of an antenna to receive a signal is inversely proportional to the frequency of the signal; as a result, short wires are better at transmitting and receiving high frequencies. Digital signals are prone to emitting RFI because logic transitions contain significant spectral components in the megahertz range. We can reduce RFI by shaping digital signals to reduce their rise/fall times. Analog circuits can also generate and receive RFI. Audio signals are at low frequencies that are less prone to interference but other types of analog circuits may operate in bands that allow them to create significant amounts of interference.

We can reduce both emissions and reception by adding shielding. A metal box provides radio frequency shielding; however, even relatively small gaps and holes in the box may leak noticeable amounts of RFI. If we can identify a part of the circuit that is receiving interfering signals, we can use a ferrite bead as a radio frequency choke to prevent the interfering signal from entering other parts of the circuit.

Crosstalk is interference between one part of a circuit and another. Crosstalk typically refers to signals carried by parasitic capacitance and inductance. The mutual capacitance between parallel wires, for example, can provide a path for significant crosstalk currents. We can use capacitance to ground to reduce the effects of crosstalk. Ground is a stable signal and a parasitic capacitance to ground can be used to overwhelm the effect of parasitics to other signals. We often construct a **ground plane** on circuit boards to help control crosstalk.

4.11 Example: Amplifying an Electret Microphone

Electret microphones [51] are widely used to pick up audio signals. The microphone itself uses permanently charged capacitor plates, one of which is flexible; audio waves that hit the microphone diaphragm cause the capacitor plate spacing to change, resulting in a change in capacitance that follows the sound pressure level.

A typical electret microphone is packaged with a transistor to provide gain as shown in Fig. 4.27. The transistor is configured in a common source configuration. However, the microphone needs external power to provide a useful signal.

Fig. 4.28 shows a simple amplifier for an electret microphone based on an op amp [12]. R_1 provides the bias current required by the microphone package. C_1 decouples the op amp input from the microphone at DC. R_4, R_5 form a voltage divider to provide a reference voltage for the op amp. R_2 provides feedback across the op amp and its value determines the gain; C_3 shorts at high frequencies, rolling off the op amp response. C_3 decouples the op amp from the output while R_5 discharges C_3 to prevent charge buildup.

To choose the values, we need to know the current drawn by the microphone, both AC and DC. The data sheet for microphones typically quotes a sensitivity value in *dbV*, or the voltage generated at 1 Pascal of air pressure. From that value, we can find the current produced by the microphone given the impedance used to make the sensitivity measurement.

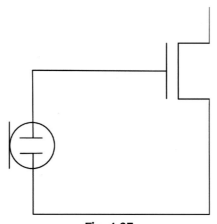

Fig. 4.27
An electret microphone package.

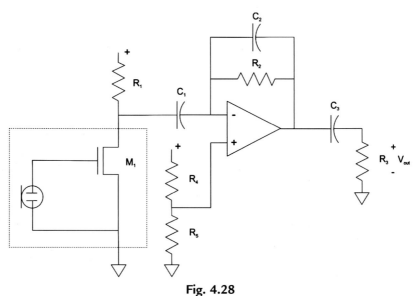

Fig. 4.28
An op amp-based electret microphone amplifier.

A typical value for the maximum AC microphone current I_{sp}—the current generated by an audio input—is in the tens of microamps. A typical maximum output voltage level for input to audio equipment would be about 1.2 V. The value of R_2 is

$$R_2 = \frac{V_{out}}{I_{sp}}. \tag{4.19}$$

The value for R_1 is set to provide the required DC bias current I_{mic} to the microphone, as given in the data sheet. We also need to know the microphone operating voltage V_{MIC}:

$$R_1 = \frac{V_{CC} - V_{MIC}}{I_S}. \tag{4.20}$$

We want the R_4, R_5 voltage divider to produce an output in the middle of the power supply voltage range to provide equal sized swings in both directions. As a result, $R_4 = R_5$. This voltage divider does not need to draw large amounts of current so we can use large-valued resistors.

We can choose a value for C_1 similar to the approach we used in Eq. (4.10), with the selected corner frequency that cuts off only very low frequencies, for example, $f_c < 10$ Hz.

The feedback capacitor C_2 helps to stabilize the op amp and forms an RC filter with R_2. We want this filter to roll off at a frequency f_p high enough to pass the desired audio band. Since R_2 and C_2 are in parallel, we can determine C_2 based on R_2 and the cutoff frequency:

$$C_2 = \frac{1}{2\pi f_p R_2}. \tag{4.21}$$

The coupling capacitor C_3 is designed with a high cutoff frequency f_{HI} to allow audio signals to pass through. It forms an RC filter with the parallel combination of R_6 and the load impedance R_L:

$$C_3 = \frac{1}{2\pi (R_6 \parallel R_L) f_{HI}}. \tag{4.22}$$

Further Reading

The **ARRL Handbook** [5] is a compendium of information on circuit design; the **ARRL RFI Book** [24] discusses radio frequency interference in detail. *IC Op-Amp Cookbook* [32] provides a comprehensive guide to op amp circuits. Prof. Marshall Leach of Georgia Tech was a highly regarded expert on analog and audio system design; his course Notes and papers can be found at https://leachlegacy.ece.gatech.edu.

Questions

Q4.1   Show the boundary between the linear and saturation regions for this set of MOSFET characteristic curves.

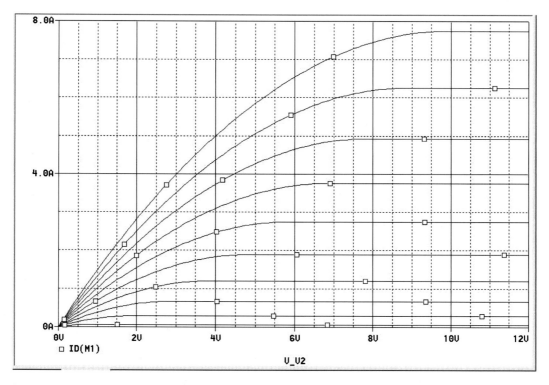

Q4.2 An amplifier input has a 100 Ω resistance in parallel with a capacitor C. What value for C gives the RC series a -3 dB cutoff frequency of $f = 20$ Hz?

Q4.3 Draw a schematic for a small-signal pi MOSFET model of a source follower amplifier.

Q4.4 A MOSFET has $g_m = 300\,{}^{\text{mA}}/_{\text{V}}$. Find its small-signal gain when used in a common source configuration with $R_S = 1$ kΩ, $R_D = 200$ Ω.

Q4.5 An inverting opamp has a feedback resistor $R_2 = 5000$ Ω. What value should the input resistor R_1 have to give a gain of -10?

Q4.6 Prove that for equal resistor values $R = R_1 = R_2 = R_3 = R_4$, the output of the op amp difference amplifier is proportional to $V_B - V_A$.

CHAPTER 5

Filters, Signal Generators, and Detectors

5.1 Introduction

Circuits operate on signals. We use circuits to generate useful signals, manipulate the signals, and interesting properties. Filters perform linear functions on signal and, for example, allow us to select ranges of frequencies in a signal. Detectors perform nonlinear operators. We will consider passive R, L, and C components; active circuits built from op amps; and digital methods.

The next section introduces the basic forms of specification for filters. Section 5.3 introduces the tank circuit and its properties. Section 5.4 discusses transfer functions; Section 5.5 considers the relationships between filter specifications and transfer functions. Section 5.6 introduces active filters using op amps. We then pause to consider a bass boost filter as an example in Section 5.7. Section 5.8 looks at advanced types of filters. Section 5.9 introduces digital filter structures. Section 5.10 considers pulse and timing circuits. Section 5.11 looks at methods to generate waveforms. Section 5.12 designs a digital arbitrary waveform generator. Section 5.13 introduces some useful detectors. Section 5.14 uses a comparator to determine when a headphone jack is inserted into a connector.

5.2 Filter Specifications

While we can specify and design all sorts of filters, four categories account for many of the filters of practical use:

- A **low-pass filter** passes low frequencies and attenuates high frequencies.
- A **high-pass filter** passes high frequencies and attenuates low frequencies.
- A **band-pass filter** passes intermediate frequencies and attenuates low and high frequencies.
- A **band-reject filter** attenuates at intermediate frequencies and passes at low and high frequencies.

In each case, we need to specify two types of regions:

- The **passband** is the band in which the filter passes signals.
- The **stopband** is the band in which the filter attenuates signals.

Embedded System Interfacing. https://doi.org/10.1016/B978-0-12-817402-9.00005-4

93

The **transition band** falls between the passband and stopband. We do not explicitly specify the transition band; its characteristics are inferred.

The most basic specification for a filter is a **filter specification diagram** which is used to describe its amplitude characteristics. An example is shown in Fig. 5.1. This example shows a low-pass filter. The y-axis represents **loss**—large values mean low output levels. The white areas of the plot are the allowable range for filter response while the gray regions are forbidden regions. The passband is specified by two parameters: A_{max} is the passband attenuation; ω_p is the maximum frequency in the passband. Similarly, the stopband is specified by A_{min} and ω_s. The region in between the passband and stopband is the **transition band**.

Any particular filter can be plotted on these axes as a line showing that filter's loss versus frequency response. As shown in Fig. 5.2, any response curve that falls in the white area meets the specification; any filter whose response curve enters the shaded areas does not meet the specification.

Fig. 5.3 shows an example diagram for a high-pass filter. In this case, $\omega_s < \omega_p$. Fig. 5.4 shows a band-pass filter diagram: the passband frequency range is $[\omega_1, \omega_2]$, the lower passband stops at ω_e, and the upper passband starts at ω_4. Fig. 5.5 shows a band-reject diagram.

Audio applications vary in their application characteristics. High-fidelity audio corresponds to a bandwidth of 20 Hz to 20 kHz. Voice-quality audio corresponds to a frequency range of 20 Hz to 4 kHz.

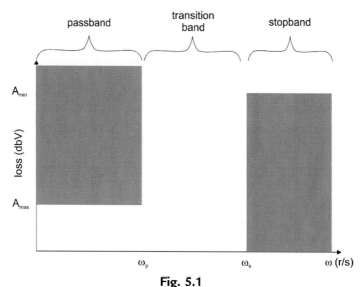

Fig. 5.1

A low-pass filter specification diagram.

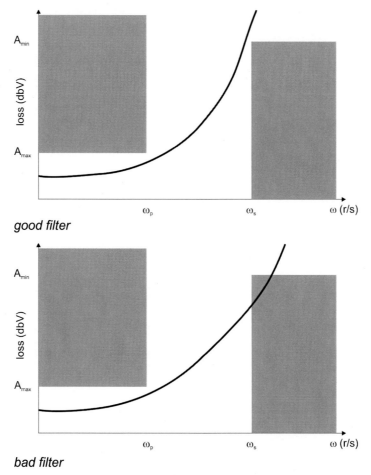

good filter

bad filter

Fig. 5.2
Filter frequency response and specification.

We may also want to specify the filter's **ripple** in the stopband, passband, or both. Some filter structures result in a ripped rather than smooth characteristic. Some applications are not particularly sensitive to ripple but in some cases we may want to specify a maximum ripple.

In some cases we may also specify phase delays at various frequencies. Audio applications are generally less sensitive to phase but digital signals can be easily distorted by phase delays.

5.3 The RLC Tank Circuit

The RLC oscillator, known as the **tank circuit**, is an important type of passive circuit. Not only is it useful in itself but its characteristics provide us with some characteristics we can use to describe filters.

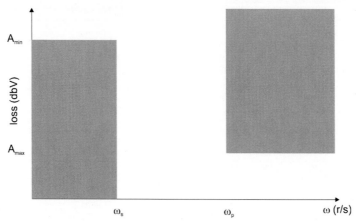

Fig. 5.3
A high-pass filter specification diagram.

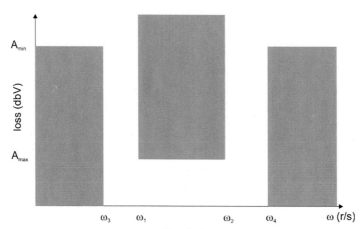

Fig. 5.4
A band-pass filter specification diagram.

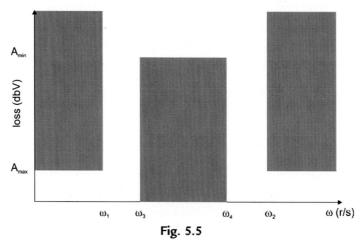

Fig. 5.5
A band-reject filter specification diagram.

Fig. 5.6
A series LC tank circuit.

Fig. 5.6 shows an ideal tank circuit consisting of an inductor and a capacitor with no resistor. The figure shows a series form of the LC tank; we can also build a parallel form. If we provide the circuit with energy—for example, by sending a pulse—the voltages and currents in the inductor and capacitor will **oscillate**. Because the circuit has no resistance, it does not dissipate energy and the tank circuit oscillates forever.

The formal name for a tank circuit is a **resonant circuit**. The frequency at which the circuit oscillates is known as its **resonant frequency**. The resonant frequency in radians per second is

$$\omega_r = \frac{1}{\sqrt{LC}}. \tag{5.1}$$

The LC circuit has infinite impedance at its resonant frequency. It appears as an open circuit at that frequency.

Fig. 5.7 shows parallel and series version of the RLC tank. Even if we do not add a discrete resistor to the circuit, capacitors and inductors have parasitic resistances; inductors are particularly prone to parasitic resistance given that they are built from coiled wires.

Fig. 5.8 shows the current and voltage waveforms for the inductor in a parallel RLC circuit. The circuit's resonant frequency is $\omega_r = 6282$ r/s or $f_r = 1$ kHz. The waveforms show the largest current at the resonant frequency and lower current values both below and above.

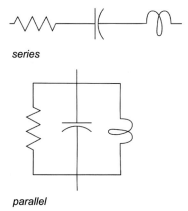

series

parallel

Fig. 5.7
Series and parallel RLC tank circuits.

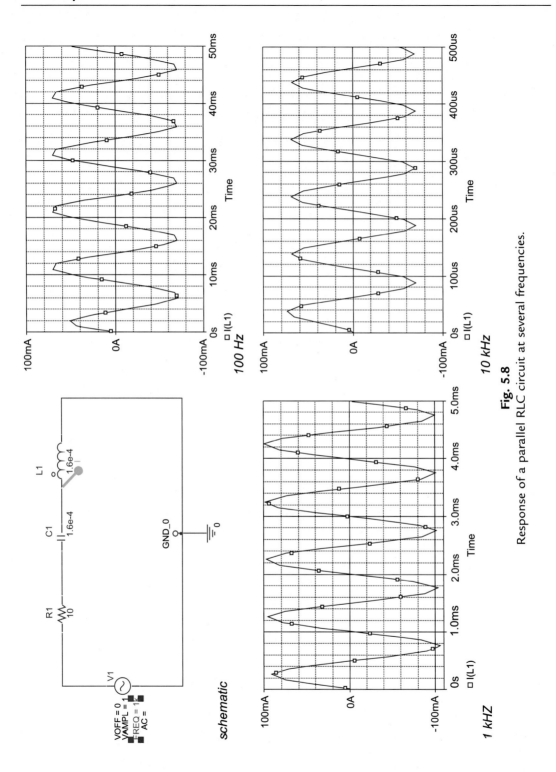

Fig. 5.8

Response of a parallel RLC circuit at several frequencies.

The RLC circuit's resistance does not change its resonant frequency but it does spread out it frequency response. The width of that curve is a measure of the circuit's **Q** or *quality*. The Q of a series RLC circuit is

$$Q_{series} = \frac{1}{R}\sqrt{\frac{L}{C}}.$$ (5.2)

The Q of a parallel RLC circuit is

$$Q_{parallel} = R\sqrt{\frac{C}{L}}.$$ (5.3)

As shown in Fig. 5.9, high-Q circuits have narrow bandwidth curves while low-Q circuits have a wide bandwidth curve. High-Q circuits are very frequency selective while low-Q circuits are less selective. If we think of the tank circuit as a band-pass filter, the high-Q circuit has a narrow passband.

The **resonant circuit bandwidth** $\Delta\omega$ is a more direct measure of the width of the frequency response:

$$\Delta\omega = \frac{\omega_r}{Q}.$$ (5.4)

As shown in Fig. 5.10, $\Delta\omega$ measures the separation between the -3 dB points on the frequency response.

5.4 Transfer Functions

As we saw in Chapter 1, the **transfer function** is a complete description of a filter's characteristics. We write the transfer function in the s domain. We can define four different transfer functions depending on what we measure at the input and output:

- The voltage-to-voltage transfer function $V_{out}(s)/V_{in}(s)$.
- The current-to-current transfer function $I_{out}(s)/I_{in}(s)$.

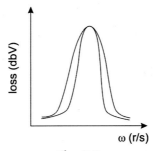

Fig. 5.9
Frequency response for high and low values of Q.

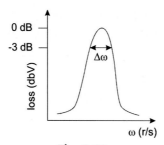

Fig. 5.10
Resonant circuit bandwidth.

- The transimpedance transfer function $V_{out}(s)/I_{in}(s)$.
- The transadmittance transfer function $I_{out}(s)/V_{in}(s)$.

Which transfer function is most appropriate depends on the nature of the source and sink attached to this circuit—whether each is best thought of in terms of voltages or currents.

Our transfer functions will be the ratio of two polynomials:

$$T(s) = \frac{a + bs + cs^2 + \cdots}{v + ws + xs^2 + \cdots}. \tag{5.5}$$

We can factor the numerator and denominator polynomials to rewrite the transfer function:

$$T(s) = K\frac{(s - z_1)(s - z_2)(s - z_3)\cdots}{(s - p_1)(s - p_2)(s - p_3)\cdots}. \tag{5.6}$$

This form exposes important structure in the transfer function. The roots of the numerator are known as **zeroes** because an s-domain frequency equal to one of the root results in a zero value for the transfer function. The roots of the denominator are known as **poles** because the transfer function becomes infinitely large at those values.

The values of the poles and zeroes determine the shape of the filter in the frequency domain. We place poles to create the passband and zeroes to create the stopband.

We can draw the poles and zeroes on the complex plane as illustrated in Fig. 5.11. Poles or zeroes on the real axis represent purely exponential behavior; poles and zeroes on the imaginary plane represent purely sinusoidal behavior; poles and zeroes elsewhere represent the product of exponentials and sinusoids. Imaginary poles come in symmetric pairs at $\pm j\omega$ values.

We require that the poles be on the right half-plane—their real component must be <0. If their real component were greater than zero, the exponential part of their behavior would have a positive coefficient, which in turn means that the function grows with time. Poles in the right half-plane correspond to negative exponentials which tend toward zero at $t = \infty$. We have no limitation on the position of zeroes—a zero can be in either the left or right half-plane.

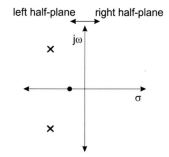

Fig. 5.11
The complex plane with poles and zeroes.

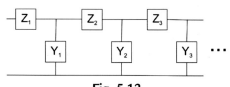

Fig. 5.12
A ladder network.

Poles and zeroes have a natural relationship to the physical behavior of the circuit. That relationship is particularly easy to see in a **ladder network**, shown in Fig. 5.12. A ladder network is built from a cascade of L-shaped elements. It is convenient to think of each element i as being made of one series impedance Z_i and a parallel admittance Y_i. If the impedance has an infinite value at some frequency ω_i then no current flows and the ladder network has a zero at that frequency. Similarly, if the admittance Y_i is infinite at some frequency, it shorts the ladder, forming a zero. Conversely, if Z_i is zero at some frequency, it forms a pole at that frequency; if Y_i is zero at some frequency, it is an open circuit that forms a pole.

While we can create an exact plot of the transfer function, in either magnitude or phase, as a function of frequency, a simple approximation of the transfer function is often enough for many purposes. The **Bode plot** method, which we introduced in Section 1.4, tells us how to create an asymptotic plot from the transfer function. The form of the body plot also gives us clues as to how to describe the transfer function.

Fig. 5.13 shows magnitude and phase Bode plots for the transfer function

$$10\frac{1+j\omega/10}{(1+j\omega/100)(1+j\omega/10000)}. \tag{5.7}$$

We can construct the asymptotic lines for the plots directly from this factored form, which has a zero at 10 rad/s and poles at 100 rad/s, 10,000 rad/s. The initial term determines the magnitude of the response. Each pole or zero forms an asymptotic line in the Bode plot: a zero forms an ascending line in magnitude and phase; a pole forms a descending line in both magnitude and

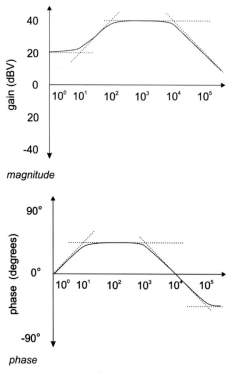

Fig. 5.13

Bode plots in magnitude and phase of a transfer function.

phase. We create the plot by taking the poles and zeros in order of frequency and building their asymptotes. The slope of each asymptote is 20 dB per decade in magnitude, 45 degrees per decade in phase. If n poles happen to be at the same location, these values are multiplied by n. As we construct the asymptotes from left to right, zeroes and poles change the slope of the asymptotic bound.

When we compare the asymptotes to the exact transfer function, we see that the actual magnitude response is 3 dB below the corner between the two asymptotic lines. If we had multiple poles or zeroes at a given frequency, the response change is multiplied by the number of poles/zeroes. Given the corner frequencies, we can quickly find the points of the frequency response at those points. From there, we can quickly sketch a more accurate representation of the frequency response. On the phase response, the transfer function goes through the asymptote at the pole/zero frequency.

The case of a pair of resonant poles is handled somewhat differently. The pair of complex poles formed by the quadratic $s^2 + as + b$ can be formed, for example, by a tank circuit. A shown in Fig. 5.14, the magnitude plot forms a peak at the resonant frequency

$$\omega_p = \sqrt{b}. \qquad (5.8)$$

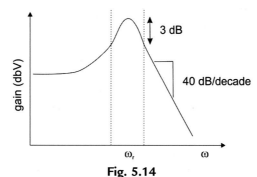

Fig. 5.14
Bode plot for a pair of complex poles.

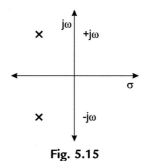

Fig. 5.15
S-domain plot for a resonant pair of complex poles.

We know from the resonant bandwidth frequency of Eq. (5.4) that the -3 dB points of the resonant response are related to Q. Those points are located at

$$\omega_p\left(1\pm\frac{2}{Q_p}\right), Q_p=\frac{\sqrt{b}}{a}. \tag{5.9}$$

Fig. 5.15 shows the resonant poles on the s plane. Their position on the vertical axis is determined by their frequency with higher frequency poles located farther from the origin. Their distance from the origin on the horizontal axis is related to the degree of damping with lower Q corresponding to a distance farther from the origin.

5.5 From Filter Specification to Transfer Function

Given a filter's specifications for passband and stopband, we can directly write the transfer function [17].

We will start with basic filters in **biquadratic** or **biquad** form to provide the form of the transfer function:

$$T(s) = K \frac{s^2 + cs + d}{s^2 + as + b}. \tag{5.10}$$

We can recast this in transfer function in terms of the filter specification parameters:

$$T(s) = K \frac{s^2 + \dfrac{\omega_z}{Q_z} + \omega_z^2}{s^2 + \dfrac{\omega_p}{Q_p} + \omega_p^2}. \tag{5.11}$$

$Q_p = \sqrt{b}/a$ was defined in Eq. (5.9); Q_z has a similar form with $Q_z = \sqrt{d}/c$.

Depending on the attenuation requirements, we may need to add poles to provide steeper filter characteristics in the transition band.

We can tailor the biquad formula to create the four basic filter types: low-pass, high-pass, band-pass, and band-reject.

In the case of the low-pass filter with passband frequency ω_p, we can write the transfer function as

$$T(s) = \frac{\omega_p^2}{s^2 + \dfrac{\omega_p}{Q_p} s + \omega_p^2}. \tag{5.12}$$

The high-pass transfer function has the form

$$T(s) = \frac{s^2}{s^2 + \dfrac{\omega_p}{Q_p} s + \omega_p^2}. \tag{5.13}$$

For both the low-pass and high-pass filters, the slope of the magnitude function from the passband to the stopband is 40 dB/decade. If we need a steeper slope to meet the stopband attenuation specification, we can add poles to increase the slope.

The band-pass transfer function has the form

$$T(s) = \frac{\dfrac{\omega_p}{Q_p} s}{s^2 + \dfrac{\omega_p}{Q_p} s + \omega_p^2}. \tag{5.14}$$

The band-reject transfer function has the form

$$T(s) = \frac{s^2 + \omega_z^2}{s^2 + \dfrac{\omega_p}{Q_p} s + \omega_p^2}. \tag{5.15}$$

where $\omega_z = \omega_p$. Each of these filter types uses a pair of complex poles to shape the filter response. The different positions of their zeroes form the shape of the filter response.

In the case of the band-pass and band-reject filters, the slope between passbands and stopbands is 20 dB/decade on each side. We can add poles to increase the slope to meet the stopband attenuation requirement.

5.6 Op Amp Filters

We can build op amp filters in several forms, all of which use feedback. We can use the noninverting and inverting forms of op amp amplifiers from Section 4.9 to build filters by using complex impedances rather than simple resistances. We can also build filters using other topologies.

Integration and differentiation are two useful functions that illustrate the use of op amp filters. Fig. 5.16 shows an integrator circuit. The feedback resistor R_f is used to prevent the DC gain from becoming infinite, given that the capacitor is an open at DC. We set $R_2 = R_1$ to correct for input bias current. The feedback impedance is

$$Z_f = R_f \parallel C_1 = \frac{R_f}{1 + sR_fC_1}. \tag{5.16}$$

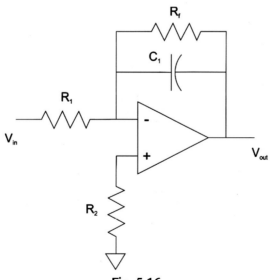

Fig. 5.16
An op amp integrator.

We know from EQ 4.14 that the transfer function of the filter is

$$T_i(s) = \frac{Z_2(s)}{Z_1(s)} = \frac{Z_f}{R_1} = \frac{R_f}{R_1} \frac{1}{1 + sR_fC_1}.$$ (5.17)

An integrator is a low-pass filter, which is consistent with this transfer function. The integrator rolls off at a frequency of $1/2\pi R_f C_1$.

Fig. 5.17 shows the *Pspice* simulation results for an op amp integrator with $R_1 = 10$ kΩ, $R_2 = 1$ kΩ, $Rf = 10$ kΩ, $C1 = 1$ nF. The figure shows both the magnitude and phase response. These plots are in the form of a Bode plot with frequency on the x-axis and log voltage output or phase on the y-axis.

The phase response of a filter can be an important aspect of its operation; we will see a simple example of the importance of phase in Section 5.7. At low frequencies, the integrator introduces a 180° phase shift; at high frequencies, it introduces less of a phase shift. The transition between these two regions is centered on the corner frequency of the filter, 10 kHz in this case.

A differentiator is a high-pass filter. Fig. 5.18 shows a differentiator circuit [41]. The basic differentiation function is provided by C_1, R_2. Both legs of the filter are built as RC sections to create a band-pass filter. Its transfer function is

$$T_d(s) = \frac{Z_2(s)}{Z_1(s)} = \frac{sC_1R_2}{(1 + sR_1C_1)(1 + sR_2C_2)}.$$ (5.18)

The low-frequency rolloff occurs at $1/2\pi R_2 C_1$. The filter has two high-frequency rolloff points. We can increase the sharpness of the cutoff by choosing the component values such that

$$\frac{1}{2\pi R_1 C_1} = \frac{1}{2\pi R_2 C_2}.$$ (5.19)

Fig. 5.19 shows the Pspice simulation output of an op amp differentiator with $R_1 = 10$ kΩ, , $C_1 = 1$ nF, $Rf = 10$ kΩ, $C_2 = 1$ nF. The output magnitude goes up with frequency, indicating that it sees more change on the input, then rolls off thanks to the feedback capacitor. The phase response has a shape similar to that of Fig. 5.17 but with different absolute values.

5.7 Example: Bass Boost Filter

Bass boost filters are commonly used to emphasize bass for audio systems. Fig. 5.20 shows the schematic for a simple bass booster that operates in two phases. The input signal goes directly to the second stage in one fork; in the other fork, it goes to a low-pass filter. As we will see shortly, we should pay attention to the phase of the low-pass filter's output. The second stage is a summing circuit that adds together the two signals.

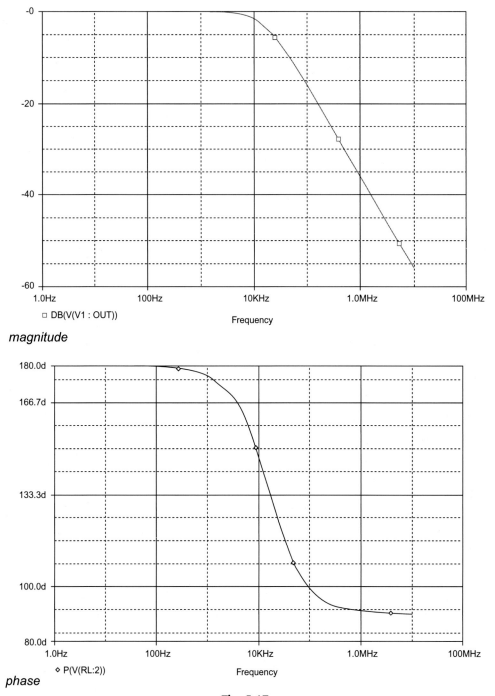

Fig. 5.17
Simulation output for a sample op amp integrator.

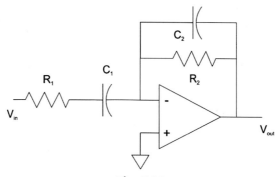

Fig. 5.18
An op amp differentiator.

Fig. 5.21 shows the *Pspice* schematic for the complete bass boost filter. The first stage is a low-pass filter with a corner frequency of $1/Rf \cdot C_1 = 20$ Hz. This op amp is configured as a noninverting amplifier so its output is in phase with its input—the output is shifted in phase but is still close in phase to the input. We want the phases of the two signals to be similar so that they do not subtract when combined. We use a summing amplifier as the final stage to combine the bass signal with the input signal; we use a fixed resistor here for simplicity.

Fig. 5.22 shows the frequency response of the bass boost filter. This simulation uses the **AC sweep mode** of *Pspice*: the input source $V1$ is a voltage source whose frequency is swept over a specified range; the output shows the dB voltage levels over that frequency range. The result is similar to a Bode plot but shows measured values rather than asymptotes. In this case, the bottom curve is the response of the first stage and the top curve is the final output. The bass boost output shows the contribution of the low-pass filter.

The second stage uses an inverting topology. The resistor tree at the negative input delivers a voltage to the negative terminal determined by the sum of the signals into the two branches of the tree. If we use equal-valued resistors in the tree and the feedback circuit, the sum is equally weighted. If we use a potentiometer at the branch fed by the low-pass filter, we can vary the amount of bass boost.

We can generalize the structure of the bass boost to create an audio equalizer as shown in Fig. 5.23. An equalizer divides the audio range into bands and provides adjustable levels in each band. This example uses three bands but more are possible. Each band has its own filter. We choose the passband frequencies for adjacent filters at the same point to provide reasonably flat coverage—the -3 dB points at the passband edge add together. We use potentiometers in the resistor tree at the final stage to control the level of each stage.

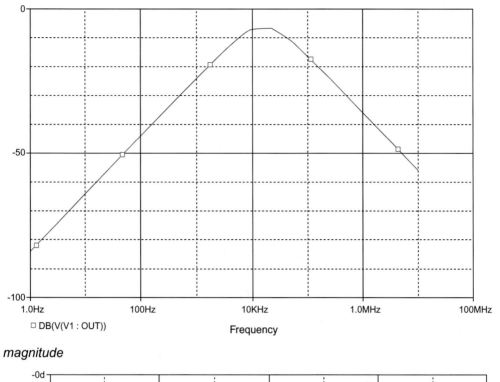

□ DB(V(V1 : OUT))   Frequency

magnitude

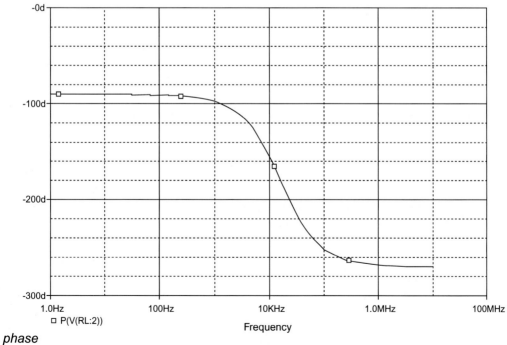

□ P(V(RL:2))   Frequency

phase

Fig. 5.19
Simulation output for a sample op amp differentiator.

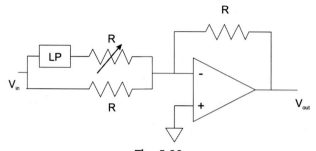

Fig. 5.20
A simple bass boost filter.

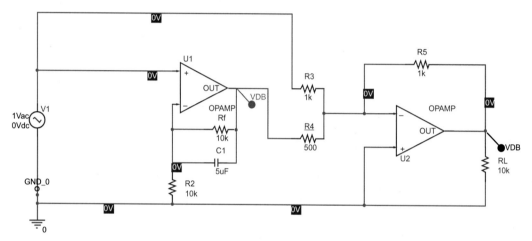

Fig. 5.21
Schematic for a bass boost filter.

5.8 Advanced Filter Types

If we are willing to move beyond the biquadratic form and allow for a larger number of poles and zeroes, we can create several different types of filters that provide more dramatic response curves. These different types of filters each has its own advantages and disadvantages. We refer to the different filter configurations as *approximations* because they approximate the characteristics of a perfect brick-wall filter. For all these filters, we can choose the order of the filter: higher order means stronger filter behavior but also more expensive implementation. Each of these approximations is formulated in terms of a low-pass filter. If we want a filter of another type, we can apply transformations from the low-pass form to the desired form.

The **Butterworth approximation** distributed the zeroes of the transfer function equally around a circle on the s plane. This results in a transfer function whose slope is maximally flat at DC. The transfer function rolls at a rate proportional to the number of zeroes. The result can be a strong drop-off from DC to the edge of the passband.

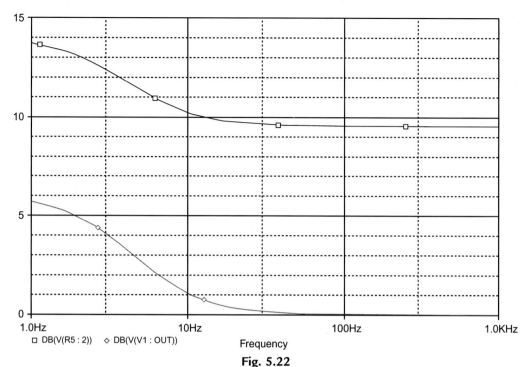

Fig. 5.22
Simulation output of the bass boost filter.

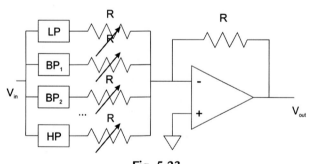

Fig. 5.23
An audio equalizer circuit.

The **Chebyshev approximation** uses ripple in the passband to achieve maximal flatness. The ripple means that the filter gain alternates between decreasing and increasing with frequency through the passband. The number of ripples is equal to the order of the filter. This configuration provides higher stopband loss than is possible with the smoother Butterworth filter. The Chebyshev zeroes are distributed along an ellipse.

The **elliptic approximation** uses a combination of poles and zeroes in the stopband to provide a maximally flat stopband. As a result, the stopband loss is closer to the specified loss, unlike the

Chebyshev filter which gives greater than required stopband attenuation. The elliptic filter is widely used due to its efficiency satisfaction of the filter specification.

Although audio applications are generally insensitive to phase, digital signals require careful control of phase characteristics. The **Bessel approximation** is used to provide a flat passband and good control of phase characteristics in the passband.

5.9 Digital Filters

Digital filters do not suffer from parasitic or temperature variations that affect analog filters. As we will see in Chapter 6, digital waveforms do suffer from sampling limitations; we must also consider numerical effects. We often use a combination of analog and digital filtering.

Digital filters can be designed in either of two forms: **finite impulse response (FIR)** or **infinite impulse response (IIR)**. IIR filters are smaller but also suffer from more numerical issues. Both are synchronous systems that operate under the control of a clock. We can build digital filters in software or directly in logic; we concentrate here on logic implementations.

Fig. 5.24 shows the structure of an FIR filter. The z^{-1} operators are unit delay operators that are implemented as registers. Coefficients b_i are multiplied along some some paths. The products are added together to produce the filter output. The structure can be written as

$$f(n) = \sum_{0 \le i \le n} b_i x(n-i).   \tag{5.20}$$

The **order** of the filter is equal to n. An FIR filter has no feedback. As a result, its impulse response is finite—if we put a unit impulse into the filter's input, the filter's output will return to zero after n cycles. The lack of feedback also means that the maximum value of a signal is limited.

Several different algorithms can be used to design the coefficients of an FIR filter from its specification including the window method and the Parks–McClellan algorithm.

Fig. 5.25 shows one type of structure that can be used for an IIR filter; other types of structures can also be used. The IIR filter includes feedback which results in the potentially time-unbounded response of the filter. IIR filters generally require less hardware than do equivalent

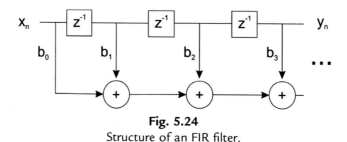

Fig. 5.24
Structure of an FIR filter.

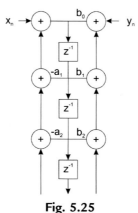

Fig. 5.25
One type of structure for an IIR filter.

filters. The coefficients of an IIR filter are generally found by transformation from an analog transfer function, for example, an elliptical approximation.

Digital filters operate on finite-sized words. We must choose word size to allow for the range of values that can be computed. The **dynamic range** of the filter depends not only on that of the input signal but also the coefficients in the filter. The dynamic range of the input signal can be represented as

$$R_{in} = [-v, +v]. \tag{5.21}$$

The most extreme values that can be generated in an FIR filter are

$$R_{out} = \left[-v \sum_{0 \le i \le n} b_i, +v \sum_{0 \le i \le n} b_i \right]. \tag{5.22}$$

IIR filters require more care since feedback means that the signal can grow to unbounded levels.

Digital filters can be built using word-parallel or word-serial arithmetic. Word-serial structures introduce latency since a single word operation takes several clock cycles. But word-serial structures can be built.

Many FPGAs include hardware multipliers in their logic elements. The combination of native multipliers and a large number of registers makes FPGAs well suited to digital filtering.

5.10 Pulse and Timing Circuits

The **LM555 timer** [19, 66], generally known as the **555 timer**, is a popular IC thanks to its versatility. It can generate pulses over as many as seven orders of magnitude of time. It can generate either a single pulse or a pulse train. It operates over a wide range of voltages and is designed to provide stable timing over a large temperature range.

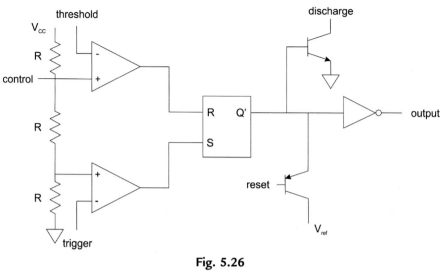

Fig. 5.26
The 555 timer.

Fig. 5.26 shows a schematic for the 555. The trigger input greater than $V_{CC}/3$ causes a pulse to be generated: the flip-flop state is set; the flip-flop drives an output stage to provide a large current to the output. When the threshold voltage reaches $2V_{CC}/3$, the flip-flop is reset. This causes the discharge transistor to be turned on—it can sink a large current. The flip-flop can also be reset with a negative pulse. A control voltage can be used to adjust the threshold.

Fig. 5.27 shows a 555 timer configured to operate as a **one shot**, also known as a **monostable multivibrator**. A trigger input causes an output pulse of a known length to be generated. One shot is widely used to condition short pulses and ensure that be sure that they satisfy a known duration. The duration of the pulse is determined by the value of capacitor C_1. A pulse causes the output to be driven high, providing a current to charge C_1. When the output voltage reaches $2V_{CC}/3$, it sets off the threshold comparator. As a result, the internal flip-flop is reset, the output drive stops, and the discharge transistor is turned on to discharge C_1. The control input is not used here; its value is maintained at C_2.

Fig. 5.28 shows the relationship between time delay and the values of C_1 and R_A. A wide range of time delays can be implemented using various combinations of component values.

5.11 Signal Generators

Fig. 5.29 shows a 555 timer configured as an **astable** or **multistable multivibrator** [66]. This circuit generates a stable train of pulses. It does so thanks to feedback—the timing capacitor is connected to the trigger. A trigger input causes C_1 to start to charge through R_A+R_B; when it reaches $2V_{CC}/3$, it triggers a discharge through R_B, which continues until the voltage reaches

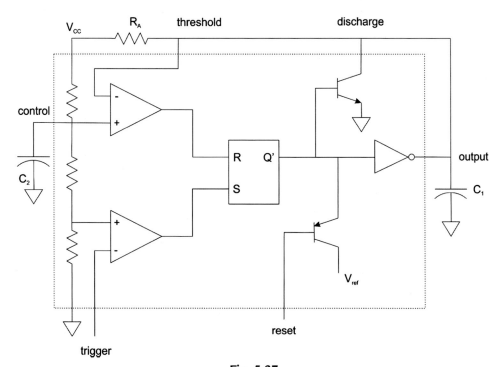

Fig. 5.27
A 555 timer configured as a one shot.

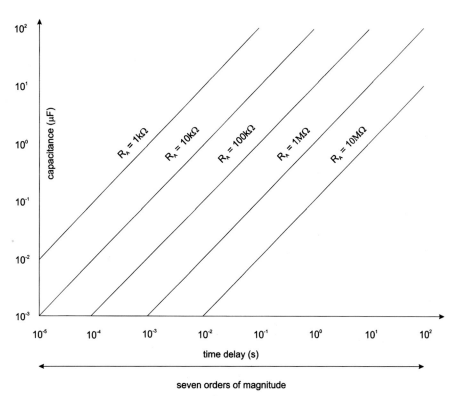

seven orders of magnitude

Fig. 5.28
555 time delay as a function of resistance and capacitance [19].

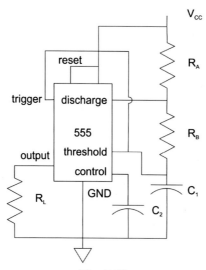

Fig. 5.29
A 555 timer configured as an astable multivibrator.

$V_{CC}/3$. Since the trigger is negative, this low voltage causes a trigger that starts another cycle. The period of the pulse is given by the sum of the charge and discharge times:

$$T = t_{chg} + t_{dis} = 0.69(R_A + R_B)C_1 + 0.69R_B C_1 = 0.69(R_A + 2R_B)C_1. \qquad (5.23)$$

The control input can be used to modify the duty cycle of the pulse. Changing the control voltage modifies the threshold voltage that determines when a pulse is triggered.

We sometimes want to generate a pulse train at a higher frequency relative to an input pulse train, for example, when we translate a low-frequency reference signal into a high frequency clock. The **phase-locked loop (PLL)** can be used to generate signals at multiples of an input frequency. As shown in Fig. 5.30, the phase-locked loop is a closed-loop control system which compares the difference in phase between the reference signal and output signal; that error signal is used to adjust the frequency of a voltage controlled oscillator (VCO). PLLs must be carefully designed to provide required accuracies but integrated PLL generators are widely available.

Triangle waves and **sawtooth waves** have a variety of uses. Triangle waves are sometimes used as substitutes for sine waves as driving waveforms. An accurate triangle wave is easier to generate than a high-quality sine wave. As shown in Fig. 5.31, a triangle waveform has

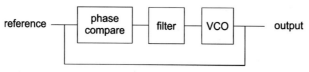

Fig. 5.30
Architecture of a phase-locked loop.

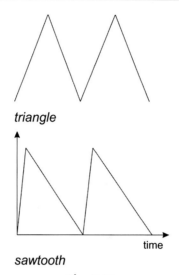

Fig. 5.31
Triangle and sawtooth waveforms.

approximately equal upward and downward slopes while a sawtooth has one side of the tooth much steeper than the other. Some authors treat the two terms as synonymous but maintaining a distinction between the two types of waveforms is useful.

We can build a sawtooth or triangle waveform generator based on the astable multivibrator. Feeding the pulse train into an op amp integrator results in a sawtooth waveform whose up and down slopes depend on the duty cycle of the pulse.

We can also generate a triangle waveform using the circuit of Fig. 5.32 [59]. The op amp O_1 is configured as an integrator and generates the triangle waveform. The two comparators C_1, C_2 determine when O_1 switches between positive and negative slope segments: C_2 causes the switch from negative to positive slope; C_1 causes the transition from positive to negative slope. The diode in the C_1 feedback loop allows it to latch its state.

We can use diodes to build circuits that generate piecewise linear approximations of waveforms. Fig. 5.33 shows a waveform and its piecewise linear approximation. Each linear segment has a characteristic slope that we will trace by changing the gain of the output amplifier. The breakpoints are represented by voltages.

Fig. 5.34 shows the waveshaper circuit [63]; additional breakpoints can be added with more diodes and resistors. The input to the circuit is a simpler waveform such as a triangle. The diodes are used to enable and disable resistors on the input leg to the op amp; by changing the input leg resistance, we modulate the gain of the op amp and change the slope of the output. We solve equations for the slopes of the curves and breakpoint values to find the values of the resistors.

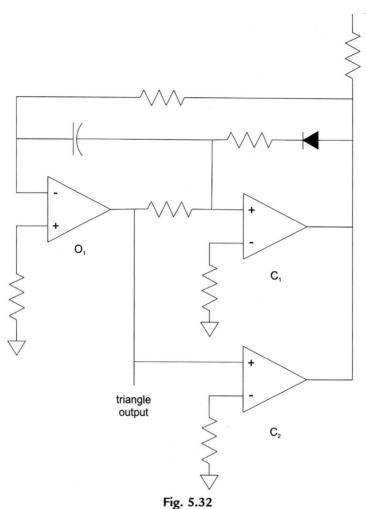

Fig. 5.32
A triangle generator waveform [59].

The slopes of the piecewise linear segments are determined by the op amp gain. Since $A_v = -R_F/R_D$ where R_D is the resistance of the input leg resistor network, enabling and disabling different resistors in the network changes the slope of the output waveform. The feedback capacitor provides a small amount of smoothing for the waveform.

The breakpoint values are determined by the voltage dividers formed by the AB pairs of resistors. At low values of V_{in}, both diodes are off and the input leg resistance is

$$R_D = (R_{1A} + R_{2A}) \parallel (R_{1B} + R_{2B}). \tag{5.24}$$

Let the voltage divider ratio $D_2 = R_{2B}/(R_{2A} + R_{2B})$. When $V_2 = V_{in}D_2 = V_A - 0.7V$, the right-hand control diodes turn on and shorts out R_{2B}, resulting in a change in the input leg resistance to the

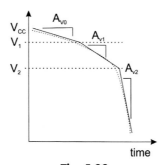

Fig. 5.33
Piecewise linear approximation of a waveform.

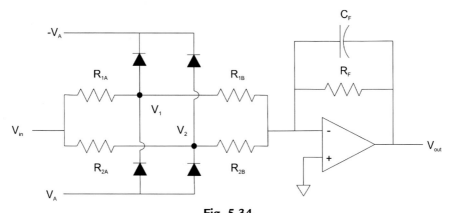

Fig. 5.34
A diode waveform shaping circuit.

op amp. Similarly, when $V_1 = V_{in} D_1 = V_A - 0.7V$, the left-hand control diodes turn on, shorts out R_{2B}, and once again changes the op amp's input leg resistance.

The standard method to build an accurate frequency reference, short of an atomic clock, is a **crystal oscillator**. Crystals exhibit the **piezoelectric effect** which trades mechanical stress and electrical oscillation: put a crystal under mechanical stress and it causes an electrical signal through it to oscillate; put an oscillatory signal into the crystal and it produces a small mechanical deformation. Crystals have two important properties that make them excellent frequency references. First, they provide a very accurate frequency that is determined by the properties of the crystal and how it is cut. Second, the crystal's behavior is stable under a broad range of environmental and operating conditions. Crystals also have very high Q.

Fig. 5.35 shows an equivalent circuit for a simple model of a crystal [5]. The crystal operates at a base frequency modeled by C_0 while the series RLC stage models harmonic imperfections. (A more accurate model would also include additional RLC stages for higher-order harmonics,

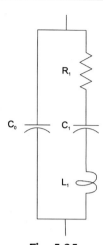

Fig. 5.35
Equivalent circuit for a crystal.

which occur at odd multiples.) Overall, the impedance of the crystal falls with increasing frequency. The crystal exhibits two resonant frequencies that are close together: one results in a low reactance while the other results in a high reactance.

Fig. 5.36 shows a crystal **Colpitts oscillator** [5]. The crystal provides an oscillatory input. The tank circuit consists of a radio frequency inductor and a pair of capacitors connected in a voltage divider.

5.12 Example: Arbitrary Waveform Generator

A digital block provides a good way to build an **arbitrary waveform generator**. This device periodically generates samples from a table; changing the table contents changes the output waveform. We will concentrate here on the digital design; the samples can be sent to an analog/digital converter for conversion to an analog waveform.

As shown in Fig. 5.37, the samples are stored in an SRAM. To simplify the design, we use it strictly as a ROM; its contents are initialized by the FPGA configuration. We could add an interface to the waveform generator to allow new sample values to be downloaded while the FPGA is powered on. The sample controller maintains a counter to cycle through the samples in the SRAM. The speed at which it generates the waveform is controlled by the clock input. A separate counter is used to provide a multiplication factor for sample generation. Given a multiplication factor of M, the sample controller waits M clock cycles between samples. The waveform generator module instantiates these two components, wires them together, and wires them to the clock and reset inputs.

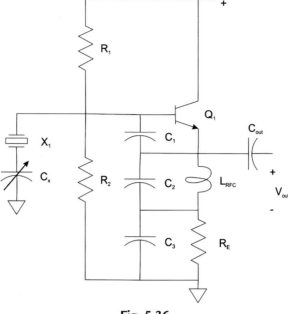

Fig. 5.36
A Colpitts crystal oscillator [5].

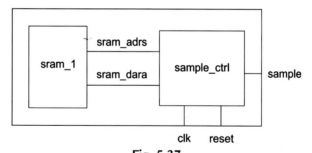

Fig. 5.37
A digital arbitrary waveform generator.

5.13 Signal Detectors

A **comparator** IC [61] is used to generate a discrete signal based on the difference of its two inputs V_+, V_-. A comparator uses a differential pair at its input, much like an op amp, but its output stage is designed to produce a discrete output, not a linear one. Unfortunately, we use the same schematic symbol for a comparator and an op amp.

We can also use op amps to compare two voltages. We are not in these cases using the linear characteristics of the op amp, but rather saturating its outputs to one or the other power supply rail. While an op amp is not specifically designed to drive logic gates, their voltage levels and

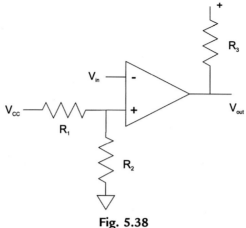

Fig. 5.38
An op amp comparator.

current output are more than enough to provide valid signals for many logic families. A comparator provides a good way to make a decision in the analog domain and translate the result to a digital value.

Fig. 5.38 shows an op amp comparator. The V_+ input is fed by a voltage divider that provides the reference voltage to which V_{in} is compared. R_3 is a pullup resistor that ensures the output goes to V_{CC} when the output is supposed to be high.

Amplitude modulation (**AM**) is used in broadcast radio and other forms of communication. As shown in Fig. 5.39, the amplitude of a **carrier signal** at a higher frequency is modulated

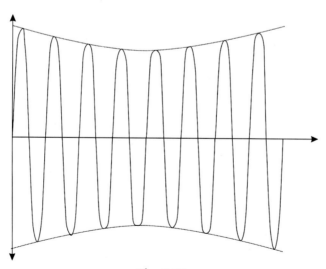

Fig. 5.39
An amplitude modulated (AM) waveform.

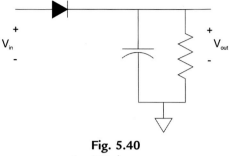

Fig. 5.40
An AM detector.

using another signal. The peak-to-peak smoothed version of the modulated signal, known as the **envelope**, traces the modulating signal. AM is used in radio because audio frequencies cannot be efficiently transmitted; the carrier signal allows for propagation at higher frequencies.

Fig. 5.40 shows an AM detector circuit, also known as an **envelope detector**. The diode provides the nonlinear element required for detection; the RC filter smooths the waveform. This circuit is very similar to the rectifier circuit we will see in Chapter 7 for AC-DC power conversion.

With the proper selection of time constants, we can use this detector to measure the envelope of other types of waveforms. Envelope values can be used, for example, as level controls. Thresholding the envelope can also provide a signal to initiate some other action.

Frequency modulation, shown in Fig. 5.41, modifies the frequency of the carrier rather than its amplitude. FM provides higher signal-noise ratios since physical noise sources tend not to disrupt the frequency modulation effect.

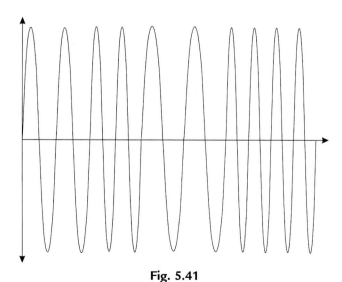

Fig. 5.41
A frequency modulated (FM) waveform.

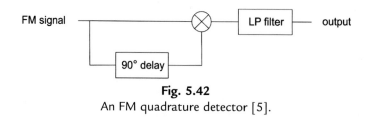

Fig. 5.42

An FM quadrature detector [5].

FM detection requires more sophisticated circuits and several different types of detectors have been invented. Fig. 5.42 shows a quadrature detector: it mixes the signal with a version of the signal that is delayed 90 degrees relative to the carrier frequency. The mixer produces several products. A low-pass filter is used to select a version of the baseband signal.

5.14 Example: Headphone Jack Detector

Comparing to a reference voltage allows us to detect events such as plugging in or unplugging a signal. A very common example is detecting when a headset has been plugged into an audio device.

Fig. 5.43 shows a circuit used to detect when external devices are plugged into a headphone port [1]. The V_- input is connected to a voltage divider formed by R_1, R_2 that generates a reference voltage; capacitor C_1 shorts out AC signals. The V_+ input has its own voltage divider formed by resistors 212 and 214; it also has a shunt capacitor to filter out transients. The R_3, R_4 voltage divider is used not only to test whether something is plugged into the port, but also with C_2 shorting out AC signals. If nothing is plugged into the port, the R_3, R_4 voltage divider directly determines the V_+ voltage.

The voltage dividers are used to define a known voltage. The comparator compares that known voltage to the voltage at the jack—if the jack voltage is higher than the reference, nothing is plugged in. We can choose the relative values of the two voltage dividers to ensure that the op amp's output will be high. If we plug a speaker into the port, its low impedance, along with the current-limiting transistor R_5, will be in parallel with R_4. As a result, the V_+ will go down to a low enough value to be below the V_- level, causing the op amp's output to switch to the opposite value. The output of the detector can, for example, be connected to one of the CPU's interrupt signals. Detecting a plug event can then signal the driver to perform the required housekeeping operations to respond to the signal.

Fig. 5.44 shows the Pspice schematic for the jack detection circuit. A MOSFET is used to model the connection and disconnection of the 8Ω speaker; a voltage pulse circuit is used to drive the MOSFET's gate and turn the transistor on and off. Fig. 5.45 shows the behavior of the circuit— when the MOSFET is on and the speaker resistance is connected to the input, the op amp output goes negative, indicating a connection.

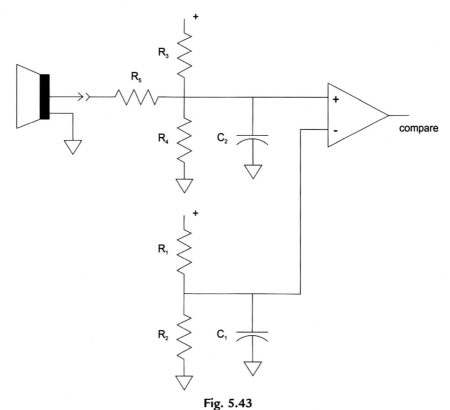

Fig. 5.43
A headphone port detection circuit.

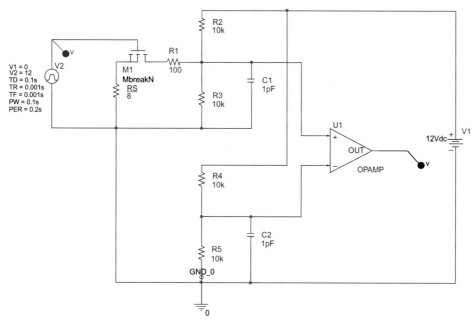

Fig. 5.44
Schematic for the jack detection circuit.

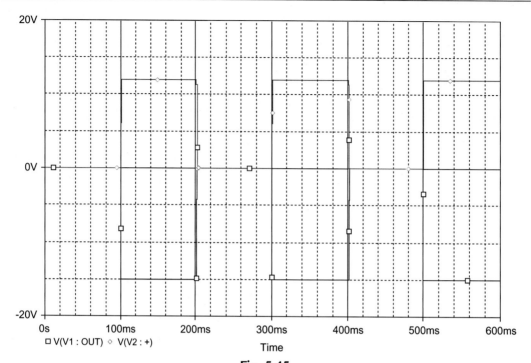

Fig. 5.45
Simulation output of the jack detection circuit.

We can build several detectors with different thresholds to detect which of several different devices has been plugged in, assuming that the different devices have sufficiently different impedances that we can reliably distinguish between them.

An example 3.5 mm headphone jack is shown in Fig. 5.46. The jack is divided into four different conducting areas separated by insulators. This arrangement, known as a **TRRS jack** for tip/ring/ring/sleeve, allows for three different signals and a ground/signal return. The ability

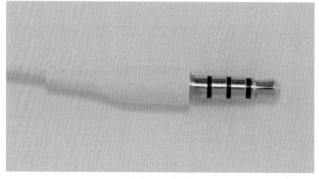

Fig. 5.46
A four-conductor headphone jack.

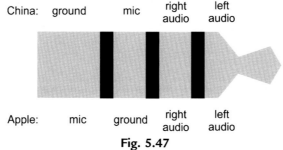

Fig. 5.47
China versus Apple configurations for TRRS jacks.

to detect multiple devices is particularly useful with modern headsets that include both microphone and speakers. First, we need to be able to distinguish between a headset that has only stereo speakers versus one that includes a microphone as well as speakers. Second, two different configurations of the four-conductor speakers-plus-microphone arrangement exist. As shown in Fig. 5.47, headphones differ as to where they put the signal return relative to the other signals. One configuration is known as the **China** headset configuration while the other is known as the **Apple** configuration. Neither configuration provides a functional advantage; the two configurations exist simply because no industry standard was developed. Since both types of headsets are in common usage, audio devices must first detect a jack insertion, then test the terminals to see which configuration is in use, then connect their internal circuits to the proper sections of the jack. The combination of connections can be sequenced using either a digital finite-state machine or a software controller.

The TPA6166A2 [65] is an audio amplifier chip that also detects when accessories are connected and their TRRS configuration. When a jack is detected as having been insertion, the chip runs an algorithm to determine its TRRS configuration; it requires two consecutive configuration operations to determine the same type for it to consider the result reliable.

Further Reading

Lancaster's Active Filter Cookbook [33] provides a thorough introduction to active filters. Jung [32] discusses a wide variety of precision op amp circuits. Daryanani [17] describes the design of op amp filters in detail. McClellan et al. [39] describe digital filters in detail.

Questions

Q5.1   Draw a filter specification diagram for a low-pass filter with $\omega_p = 4k$, $\omega_s = 5k$, $A_{max} = 3$ dB, $A_{min} = 50$ dB.

Q5.2   Draw a filter specification diagram for a high-pass filter with $\omega_p = 10$ k, $\omega_s = 8$ k, $A_{max} = 1$ dB, $A_{min} = 60$ dB.

Q5.3   Draw a filter specification diagram for a band-pass filter with $[\omega_1, \omega_2]=[1k, 4k]$, $[\omega_3, \omega_4]=[500, 5k]$, $A_{max}=3$ dB, $A_{min}=50$ dB.

Q5.4   Draw a filter specification diagram for a band-reject filter $[\omega_1, \omega_2]=[2k, 10k]$, $[\omega_3, \omega_4]=[1.5k, 10k]$, $A_{max}=1$ dB, $A_{min}=50$ dB.

Q5.5   Draw a Bode plot for a low-pass filter with a gain of 20 dB at $\omega=0$ and one pole at $\omega=2k$r/s.

Q5.6   Draw a Bode plot for a high-pass filter with a pole at $\omega=0$, gain of zero at $\omega=0$, and one pole at $\omega=2k$r/s.

Q5.7   A series RLC circuit has $R=1$ kΩ, $L=1$ μH, $C=1$ μF.

   (a)   What is its resonant frequency ω_r?

   (b)   What is its Q?

Q5.8   Give a biquadratic transfer function for a low-pass filter with $\omega_p=4k$, $Q_p=25$.

Q5.9   Give a biquadratic transfer function for a high-pass filter with $\omega_p=10k$, $Q_p=50$.

Q5.10 Find feedback component values for an active RC low-pass filter with $R_1=R_f=1$ kΩ, $f_p=5$ kHz.

CHAPTER 6

Analog/Digital and Digital/Analog Conversion

6.1 Introduction

Converting between digital and analog signals is key to our ability to use digital computers to process analog data. To complete the loop between the external world and our computer, we need both **analog/digital converters** (**ADCs**) and **digital/analog converters** (**DACs**). We generally rely on integrated circuits for both ADCs and DACs; we rarely design our own. But a basic understanding of the design principles underlying converters helps us to make the best use of integrated converters.

The next section considers the rate at which we must sample analog signals to preserve their information in the digital signal. Based on this knowledge, Fig. 6.3 introduces the specifications for converters. Fig. 6.4 develops the basic method for digital/analog conversion while Fig. 6.5 looks at several different architectures for analog/digital conversion. Fig. 6.6 walks through a simple design of small analog/digital and digital/analog converters.

6.2 The Nyquist Rate

Digital signals are **sampled** from continuous analog signals. We know the value of the original continuous signal only at certain times. We want to be able to reconstruct the original continuous signal from the digital signal. In order to do so reliably, the signal must have limited bandwidth—its frequency components must be no greater than some known frequency f_c. We must then sample the signal at a minimum rate known as the **Nyquist rate**.

Fig. 6.1 shows a sinusoidal signal and samples taken at two different rates. Given samples at the Nyquist rate, we can reconstruct the original sine wave. If we sample at a lower rate, we can interpolate a signal at a lower frequency that fits all of the sample points. We can, in fact, interpolate an unbounded number of sinusoids at various frequencies. Most of those interpolated signals are wrong. This effect is known as **aliasing**. Fig. 6.2 illustrates the effect of aliasing in the frequency domain. The spectrum of the signal is folded along the sub-Nyquist frequency rate. Signals at frequencies slightly higher than the sampling rate appear as aliases that are slightly lower than the sample rate. Signals farther away from the sample

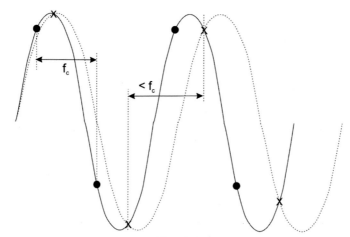

Fig. 6.1
Sampling at and below the Nyquist rate.

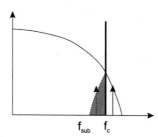

Fig. 6.2
Aliasing in the frequency domain.

rate result in aliases at even lower frequencies. Aliasing causes distortion in our original signal that cannot be removed—we do not know which part of the sampled signal is actual and which is aliased.

6.3 Conversion Specifications

Conversion speed is an important metric. While DACs can operate at very high speeds, ADCs vary greatly in their conversion speed for a given number of bits.

We are concerned with two types of noise in conversion. **Quantization noise** is the result of the finite representation of samples. The simplest form of representation is linear—the sample value is a linear function of the signal value. Given an n bit representation of signal $x \in [0, V]$, we have a step size

$$\Delta = \frac{V}{2^n}.$$ (6.1)

The quantization noise for the sample s is

$$N_s = \frac{1}{2}\Delta. \tag{6.2}$$

The mean squared error for quantization is

$$MSE = \frac{\Delta^2}{12}. \tag{6.3}$$

Adding one bit to the representation decreases noise by 1/4 or 6 dB. The signal-to-noise ratio (SNR) of an ideal analog-digital converter is

$$20\log\frac{RMS(V_{in})}{RMS(N_s)}. \tag{6.4}$$

Given characteristics of the signal, we can determine $RMS(N_s)$.

We do not need to be limited to a linear conversion function. Some converters make use of nonlinear conversion laws as a form of data compression. The μ-law used in telecommunication is one example. Fig. 6.3 compares linear and μ-law characteristics. The μ-law, which is defined over 8-bit values, takes advantage of the semilogarithmic response of the human auditory system to use larger steps at lower volumes and smaller steps at higher volumes. The continuous form of μ-law is [9]

$$F(x) = sgn(x)\frac{\ln(1+\mu|x|)}{\ln(1+\mu)}, \; -1 \le x \le 1, \tag{6.5}$$

where $\mu = 255$ in the United States and Japan. The A-law is used in Europe:

$$
\begin{aligned}
F(x) &= sgn(x)\frac{A|x|}{1 + \ln A}, \;\; 0 \le |x| < \frac{1}{A}, \\
&= sgn(x)\frac{1 + \ln(A|x|)}{1 + \ln A}, \;\; \frac{1}{A} \le |x| < 1.
\end{aligned}
\tag{6.6}
$$

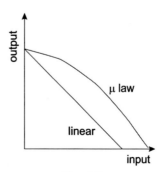

Fig. 6.3
Linear and μ-law characteristics.

Clock jitter noise is another important source of conversion noise. Phase changes in the conversion clock cause the time separation between samples to be nonuniform. As a result, slightly different samples of the signal will be taken. Clock jitter can be modeled as a Gaussian process.

In addition to noise, we must also be concerned with the accuracy of the conversion circuits. A number of circuit issues can cause the converter's output to be biased in one direction or the other.

6.4 Digital/Analog Conversion

Digital/analog conversion is in some ways the simpler conversion problem. Accurate conversion requires attention to detail but the basic principle is remarkably simple. Fig. 6.4 shows an **R-2R network** that can be used to convert bit-valued voltages to an analog voltage. The bit values are applied to the $2R$ resistors at the top. The resistor network sums the bit voltages with power-of-two weighting to form the analog output. This resistor tree can be built to any number of bits to provide arbitrary dynamic ranges.

The R-2R network is scalable to different bit widths because the first i bits always have the same impedance. Consider the impedance at point a: the effect impedance of the series 2R resistors is R. At point b, the network is equivalent to two R-valued resistors in series, giving an equivalent resistance of 2R. So at point c, the network appears to be the same as it did at point a—a series connection of two 2R resistors.

The R-2R ratio scales bits in the powers of two required for conversion. When b_0 is high, the voltage at point c is $V_{CC}/4$. If b_1 is also high, the resistor tree produces $V_{CC}/4 + V_{CC}/2$. The voltage at the output as a function of the number of stages is

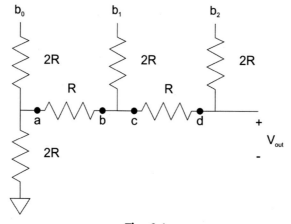

Fig. 6.4
An R-2R network.

$$V_{out} = \sum_{0 \le i \le n-1} b_i \frac{V_{CC}}{2^{n-i}}. \tag{6.7}$$

The maximum voltage that can be produced by the converter is

$$V_{max} = V_{CC}\left(1 - \frac{1}{2^n}\right). \tag{6.8}$$

DACs can operate at very high speeds given the simplicity of the network.

Accurate digital/analog conversion requires precise values for the resistors and minimal variation from resistor to resistor in the network. Converters use thin-film resistors to ensure that the resistors maintain a tight tolerance.

A more modern DAC architecture is based on **current steering**. As shown in Fig. 6.5, a set of current sources can be switched into or out of the conversion operation based on the input value. The summed currents can be transformed into a voltage using an op amp circuit.

6.5 Analog/Digital Conversion

ADCs provide a much wider range of design trade-offs. Analog-to-digital conversion methods vary widely in their speed, precision, and accuracy.

A key element in any ADC is the **sample-and-hold circuit**. As shown in Fig. 6.6, it has a simple structure: an access transistor guards a capacitor. MOSFETS provide good isolation between the sampling control signal *samp* and the sample voltage V_{samp}. The details of the circuit must be carefully designed. The access transistor must turn on and off quickly. Its on-resistance must be very low and its off-resistance must be very high. The control signal to the access transistor must also provide very sharp transitions to minimize the time for which the transistor is partially on.

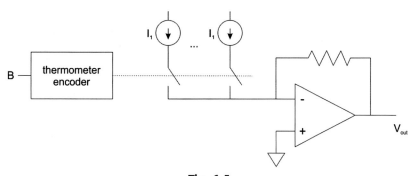

Fig. 6.5
A current steering digital/analog converter.

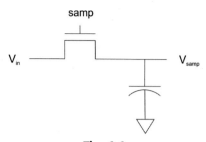

Fig. 6.6
A sample-and-hold circuit.

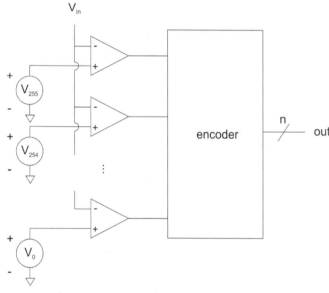

Fig. 6.7
A flash converter.

The simplest form of ADC is the **flash converter** shown in Fig. 6.7. The sample held in the sample-and-hold is sent simultaneously to 2^n comparators (in this case, 256 comparators). Each comparator has its reference value set to one of the possible quantized voltages. All the converters whose references are below the input voltage produce a 1 output; all the converters with reference voltages below the input voltage produce a 0. A logic network can be used to recode these bits into an n-bit number. Flash converters provide the highest conversion speed of any ADC architecture; they are typically used for video conversion where high speed is required. But they are expensive—the number of converters is exponential in the bit width of the output.

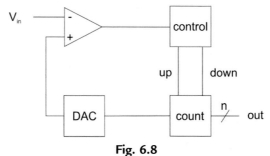

Fig. 6.8
A successive approximation ADC.

At the other end of the spectrum is the **successive approximation converter** shown in Fig. 6.8. This converter compares the sample-and-hold value to a candidate voltage held in an internal capacitor. It performs binary search to assign each bit of the digital value moving from the most-significant to the least-significant bit. At each step i, the converter compares the candidate voltage to the input voltage. If the candidate voltage is below the input voltage, then the internal DAC generates a voltage of $V_{CC}/2^{n-i}$ to add to the internal capacitor and $o_{n-1} = 1$; if the candidate voltage is already above the input voltage then nothing is added to the internal capacitor and $o_{n-1} = 0$. After n estimation steps, the value of each bit has been determined. The successive approximation converter is slow but requires only a small amount of hardware.

Fig. 6.9 shows the architecture of a **dual-slope converter**. This converter uses an interesting approach that provides high precision. An internal capacitor is charged to a voltage equal

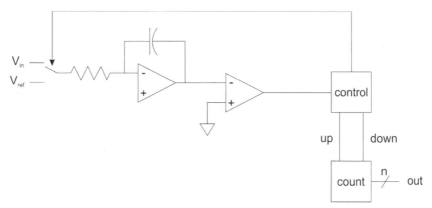

Fig. 6.9
A dual-slope ADC.

to that of the sample-and-hold voltage. The internal capacitor is then discharged at a known rate; a timer counts the amount of time required to discharge the capacitor. The final timer value is equal to the digital conversion output. Because the capacitor is both charged and discharged, many nonlinearities are canceled out, resulting in a highly linear conversion throughout the conversion range.

6.6 Example: R-2R Digital/Analog Converter

Fig. 6.10 shows the schematic for a 3-bit R-2R conversion circuit. The resistors are connected to pulse sources that are designed to produce a binary-coded output from 0 to 7. Fig. 6.11 shows the output of the R-2R network.

Fig. 6.12 shows the output of the network with some mismatched resistors: $R2 = 2$ kΩ, $R6 = 1.5$ kΩ. The mismatched values affect the results of the bits to which they are attached.

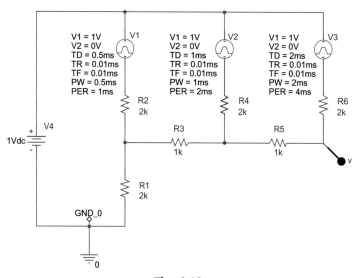

Fig. 6.10

Simulation schematic for an R-2R digital/analog converter.

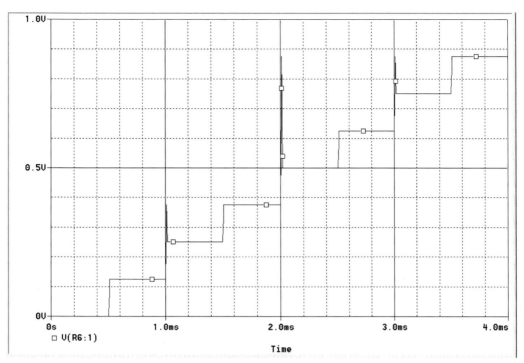

Fig. 6.11
Output of the R-2R circuit.

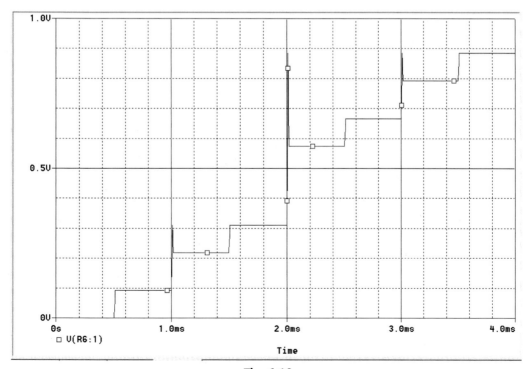

Fig. 6.12
Output of the R-2R circuit with mismatched resistors.

Questions

Q6.1   An AM signal occupies the band [600 kHz, 610 kHz].
   (a)   What sample rate is required for this signal?
   (b)   The AM signal is converted down to baseband so that its bandwidth starts at DC.
         What sample rate is required?

Q6.2   A signal occupies the band [0 Hz, 20 kHz]. It is sampled at 35 kHz. At what
       frequency does each of these components appear in the sampled signal?
   (a)   15 kHz

   (b)   18 kHz

   (c)   19 kHz

Q6.3   These samples correspond to a sinusoid at the Nyquist rate:

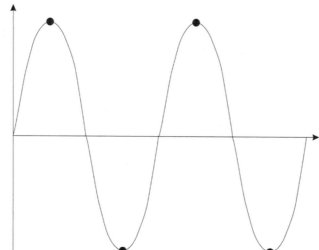

       Draw a second sinusoid at a higher frequency that can be represented by these
       samples.

Q6.4   You are given this three-bit R-2R digital/analog conversion network.

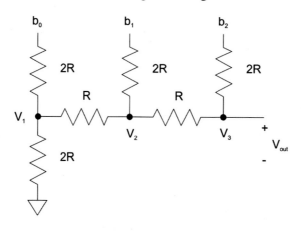

A logic 1 at each bit is represented by voltage V. Give the voltages at V_1, V_2, V_3 for each of these inputs:

(a) $b_2b_1b_0 = 101$
(b) $b_2b_1b_0 = 011$
(c) $b_2b_1b_0 = 110$

Q6.5   How many clock cycles are required for an 8-bit successive approximation DAC?

CHAPTER 7

Power

7.1 Introduction

The power supply is the unheralded hero of circuit design. The importance of a high-quality power supply becomes apparent only when we try to use a bad power supply. We sometimes build our own power supply. As with most types of circuits, a solid understanding of their design helps us to choose the proper power supply even when we use a prebuilt supply.

The next section considers the specifications for a power supply. Section 7.3 analyzes the design of AC-to-DC power supplies. Section 7.4 looks at the design of DC-DC power converters. Section 7.5 discusses batteries as power supplies. Section 7.6 designs a simple AC-to-DC power supply using discrete components. Section 7.7 considers thermal characteristics of electronics and heat dissipation. Fig. 7.8 discusses power management.

7.2 Power Supply Specifications

The most basic specification of a DC power supply is its **output voltage** and **maximum output current**. The maximum output current is typically specified relative to a load impedance. Many power supplies provide several different output voltages all derived from a common core.

Output voltage ripple is a very important specification for digital and particularly for analog circuits. Ripple does not have to be periodic; in this case, it refers to any variation in the output voltage. While digital circuits tend to be relatively insensitive to power supply voltage, large amounts of ripple may cause errors. Analog circuits are particularly sensitive to power supply ripple. Since output voltages are produced relative to the power supply, variations in the power supply result in variations in those outputs.

Conversion efficiency measures the ratio of power delivered to the load to the total power consumed by the power supply. As shown in Fig. 7.1, efficiency varies with the power delivered to the load. Most power supplies are less efficient at low loads—the overhead power consumption of the supply generally does not scale well with load power.

Heat dissipation is an important metric that may determine the case used for the system or whether it needs some form of active cooling such as a fan. Power supplies do not always directly specify their heat output. However, we do know that for a given power output, more efficient power supplies will produce less heat.

Embedded System Interfacing. https://doi.org/10.1016/B978-0-12-817402-9.00007-8

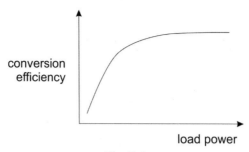

Fig. 7.1
Power supply conversion efficiency versus power delivered to the load.

The ground voltage is often used as a reference voltage throughout the circuit. The term *ground* is not chosen arbitrarily. A true **earthed ground** is directly connected to the Earth through a low-resistance connection. The voltage of the Earth is very difficult to change—Gauss's Law tells us that any charge sent to the earthed ground will be equally distributed across the surface of the Earth. Since a great deal of charge is required to noticeably change the voltage of the Earth, it provides a very good reference voltage.

Power supplies for mixed-signal systems generally provide a separate analog ground that is distinct from the digital ground. Digital signals can generate large swings that produce variations from the nominal ground voltage. Since analog signals are particularly sensitive to power supply noise, we want to isolate the analog circuits from noise created by the digital circuits.

Safety is a critical requirement for power supplies. Shocks from AC utility lines can be fatal. Improper design of power supplies can lead to fires. Even low voltages can damage other devices. We must carefully design power supplies to minimize their risk of dangerous operation and failure.

Batteries require some specialized specifications; we will defer their discussion to Section 7.5.

7.3 AC-to-DC Power Supplies

As shown in Fig. 7.2, an AC-to-DC power supply operates in four stages. The **transformer** stage transforms AC from one voltage to another. The **rectifier** stage converts the AC voltage from voltages both above and below ground to a waveform that is always nonnegative. The **filter** stage filters the rectified waveform into a DC waveform with ripple. The **regulator** stage reduces the ripple of the waveform.

A transformer is a pair of coupled conductors. The transformer windings are generally made around a metal core to increase their efficiency. The two windings are known as the **primary**

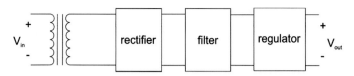

Fig. 7.2
Architecture of an AC-to-DC power supply.

winding at the input and the **secondary** winding at the output. The secondary voltage is determined by the ratio of primary to secondary windings:

$$V_s = V_p \frac{N_s}{N_p}.$$ (7.1)

We can rectify the AC waveform using either **half-wave** or **full-wave** rectification. Fig. 7.3 shows examples of each: The half-wave rectified waveform includes only half of each sinusoid; the full-wave rectified version flips the lower half of each sinusoid.

As shown in Fig. 7.4, a diode is sufficient for half-wave rectification. The lower half of the waveform is cut off by the diode when it is in its reverse bias region. In the forward bias region, it conducts the AC waveform. Full-wave rectification makes use of a **diode bridge** shown in

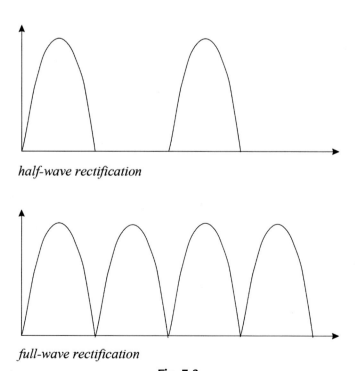

half-wave rectification

full-wave rectification

Fig. 7.3
Half-wave and full-wave rectification.

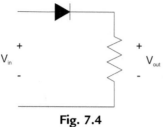

Fig. 7.4
A half-wave rectifier.

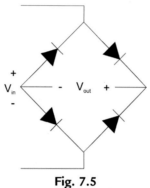

Fig. 7.5
A full-wave rectifier.

Fig. 7.5. The output of the rectifier is taken from its two interior terminals. On the positive side of the input waveform, one pair of diodes conducts; on the negative side, the other diode pair conducts. This clever configuration flips the negative half of the waveform to create the full-wave rectified waveform. A full-wave rectifier is much more efficient than the half-wave version because the half-wave rectifier throws away half of the waveform.

One or more capacitors are used to filter the rectified waveform as shown in Fig. 7.6. The capacitor acts as a low-pass filter on the rectified waveform. The larger the capacitor, the lower

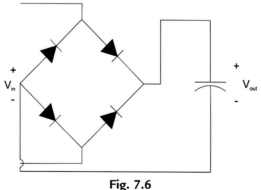

Fig. 7.6
A capacitive filter stage.

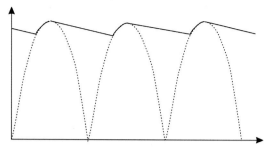

Fig. 7.7
A filtered rectified sinusoid.

the ripple. After the rectified waveform reaches its maximum value, the filter capacitor is discharged at a constant rate by the load current as shown in Fig. 7.7.

We can find the ripple at the filter output for a given load current I_L. As shown in Fig. 7.8, the voltage moves between V_H and V_L with $2V_R = V_H - V_L$. The ripple waveform has a period equal to half of the sinusoid period:

$$t_1 + t_2 = \frac{T}{2}. \tag{7.2}$$

A simple estimate for the ripple voltage is given by the capacitor law:

$$I_L = -C\frac{\triangle V}{\triangle t}; \tag{7.3}$$

$$V_R = \frac{I_L t_2}{2C} \approx \frac{I_L T}{4C}. \tag{7.4}$$

A more accurate estimate comes from finding the intercept between the current discharge ramp and the sinusoid:

$$V_L = V_H \cos\theta; \tag{7.5}$$

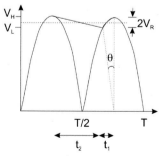

Fig. 7.8
Estimating ripple in the filtered power supply.

$$\theta = \cos^{-1}\left(1 - \frac{2V_R}{V_H}\right). \tag{7.6}$$

Since

$$\frac{\theta}{2\pi} = \frac{t_1}{T}, \tag{7.7}$$

we find

$$t_1 = \frac{T}{2\pi}\cos^{-1}\left(1 - \frac{2V_R}{V_H}\right). \tag{7.8}$$

We can use this value for t_1 to find an improved value for V_R:

$$V_R = \frac{I_L\left(^T/_2 - t_1\right)}{2C}. \tag{7.9}$$

Power supply filter capacitors must be rated to withstand high voltages. Electrolytic capacitors are generally used for the filter stage. We generally connect **bleeder resistors** across the filter capacitors to bleed off current when the power supply is off; the bleeder resistors have high resistance values to avoid draining too much current during operation.

We can use either linear or switching regulators to reduce the ripple produced at the final output. A simple **linear regulator** is shown in Fig. 7.9. This circuit uses a **Darlington pair** as a series regulation transistor Q_1.

A **Zener diode** is often used to create the reference voltage source. A Zener diode is designed to be operated in reverse bias; unlike standard diodes, they do not break down due to reverse bias current. The reverse bias voltage can be controlled by manufacturing, which allows Zener diodes to be manufactured in a wide range of stock reference voltages.

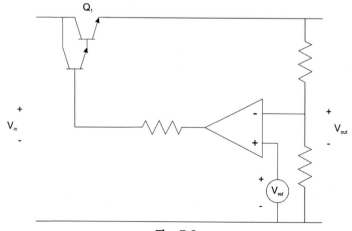

Fig. 7.9
A linear power supply regulator.

A voltage divider is used to measure the output voltage that is compared to the reference voltage. The voltage divider resistors are chosen based on the Zener diode reference voltage chosen. The Zener diode controls the regulation transistor. When the output is below the reference voltage, the regulation transistor supplies current proportional to the difference between the output and reference voltage. When the output is above the reference voltage, the regulation transistor is off, allowing the power supply output to droop as it supplies current to the load.

We can also build **switching regulators** that perform on-off control of the output voltage. A comparator is used to compare the output voltage to a reference value. The regulation transistor is used in switching mode rather than linear mode. Switching regulators provide higher efficiency than do linear regulators. But switching regulators must be carefully designed to avoid oscillation.

Many power supplies make use of integrated regulators, which provide good power quality as well as protection and other features. The LM340 [40] is a common three-terminal power regulator. It can be used as a fixed regulator by connecting capacitors to its input and output. The output voltage can be adjusted by replacing the output capacitor with a voltage divider. It can be used as a current regulator by using a resistor to turn the output current into a voltage for regulation. The LTC 3780 [34] combines buck and boost converters to provide DC-DC conversion at voltages both below and above the input voltage.

7.4 Power Converters

Power converters are used to convert one DC voltage level to another; the term is also used for DC-to-AC converters. While a power supply may be designed to supply several different voltage levels, we often make use of voltage converters to supply a specialized voltage for part of the circuit rather than find a power supply that provides all the required voltages.

Three common types of switching power converters are the **buck converter** (which converts a higher voltage to a lower one) and the **boost converter** (which converts a lower voltage into a higher one) and the **flyback converter** (which can be designed to supply multiple voltages). All these converters are nonlinear regulators; they are very efficient but also require careful design to avoid feedback-induced instability.

Fig. 7.10 shows a buck converter circuit [36]. We close the switch during the on portion of the duty cycle t_{on}, $0 \leq D = t_{on}/(t_{on}+t_{off}) \leq 1$. When the switch is closed, the inductor is energized with current. The charging current through the inductor increases with time as given by the inductor law:

$$\frac{V_L}{L} = \frac{V_{in} - V_{out}}{L} = \frac{dI_L}{dt}.$$
(7.10)

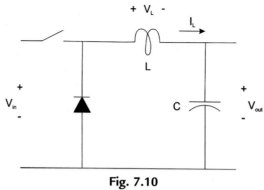

Fig. 7.10
A buck power converter.

The current waveform is a ramp whose maximum value is

$$I_{max} = \frac{t_{on}(V_{in} - V_{out})}{L}. \tag{7.11}$$

When the switch is turned off, the inductor current discharges into the capacitor. The diode provides current continuity. The current decreases at a rate

$$\frac{dI_L}{dt} = -\frac{V_L}{L} = -\frac{V_{in} - V_{out}}{L}. \tag{7.12}$$

The inductor current goes to zero when the voltage across the inductor reaches zero. The net change in voltage across the inductor over the duty cycle is zero. While the slopes of the charge and discharge waveforms may differ, we know that the charge and discharge phases balance:

$$V_{in}t_{on} = (V_{out} + V_{in})t_{off}. \tag{7.13}$$

Rewriting,

$$V_{in}\frac{t_{on}}{t_{on} + t_{off}} = V_{out} = DV_{in}. \tag{7.14}$$

The analysis of the boost converter, shown in Fig. 7.11, is similar, but in that case $V_{in}\, t_{on} = V_{out}\, t_{off}$.

As shown in Fig. 7.12, a flyback regulator makes use of a transformer. (The term *flyback transformer* comes from the cathode ray tubes used in early television, where it was used to generate the sawtooth waveform used to return the cathode ray across the screen.) The winding ratio of the transformer determines the relationship between the input and output voltage. The dots on the transformer indicate that its windings provide opposite polarities. The *ctrl* input is a pulse width modulated signal that switches the transformer primary on and off. When the

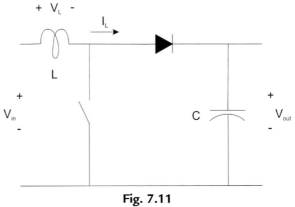

Fig. 7.11
A boost power converter.

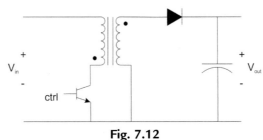

Fig. 7.12
A flyback power converter.

primary is on, the diode prevents secondary current from charging the capacitor. When the primary is off, the energy stored in the secondary is used to charge the output capacitor. We can provide several different power supplies using a transformer with multiple secondary windings, each with its own winding ratio and connected to its own diode and capacitor.

7.5 Batteries

An electrochemical **cell** can provide electrical energy to a circuit. A **battery** is a group of electrically connected cells, but we often use the term *battery* to describe any electrochemical storage device.

The most basic characteristic of a battery is its **capacity**, measured in Amp-hours. The battery's C rate is equal in value to its capacity; designers sometimes scale charge and discharge currents by C. The **energy density** of a battery describes its capacity per unit weight.

Fig. 7.13 shows a typical battery discharge curve [53] which we can use to understand some other battery specifications. As the battery is used to supply power, its voltage drops slowly.

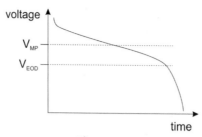

Fig. 7.13
A typical battery discharge curve.

The **midpoint voltage** V_{MP} is at the middle of the battery's operating region and is used to characterize the battery. The slope of the discharge region varies considerably for different types of batteries. As the battery nears its discharge limits, its voltage drops much more quickly. The **end-of-discharge voltage** V_{EOD}, also known as the **end-of-life voltage**, marks the point at which the battery ends its useful discharge.

A battery has an **equivalent series resistance** that limits its peak current. The **self-discharge** rate of the battery determines the length of time over which it will hold a charge.

The details of battery specifications vary widely with the **battery chemistry**. A number of different chemistries have been developed over a period of several centuries. **Alkaline batteries**, for example, are commonly used in devices that make use of replaceable batteries. The most common chemistries for **rechargeable batteries** in electronics are **nickel-cadmium (NiCD)**, **nickel-metal hydride (NiMH)**, and **lithium ion (LiIon)**.

When discharging a battery, we can monitor voltage to determine when the battery is about to reach its end-of-discharge voltage. Many battery management ICs provide signals that indicate when the battery has reached the **dropout voltage** at which the battery is no longer useful without recharging.

Recharge schemes can be classified into three categories [75]:

• **Trickle charging** provides a low discharge current.
• **Constant voltage charging** operates at a constant battery voltage.
• **Constant current charging** provides a constant charge current.

The exact type of recharge cycle required for a battery depends on its chemistry. A LiIon charging cycle starts with a precharge trickle charging phase, followed by constant current fast charging, and finally a constant voltage taper charge [2]. Fast charging—charging at high C values—can damage a battery by generating excessive heat. Fast chargers must sense when the battery is fully charged and switch to a slow charging mode to avoid damage to the battery; the end of the charging cycle is often determined by a combination of voltage and temperature [54].

Fast charging rates can also cause the battery to charge less fully as the chemical processes for charging vary with charge rate.

7.6 Example: Linear Regulated Power Supply

An AC-to-DC power supply designed to regulate 120 V introduces notable safety risks. We can safely explore power supply circuits using *Pspice*. We will build up a linear regulated supply in stages.

Fig. 7.14 shows the schematic of a simple circuit with a transformer and full-wave rectifier. The transformer is specified with a 1:10 ratio of primary to secondary windings to reduce the 120 V input to 12 V. The transformer secondary is connected to the full-wave rectifier. Fig. 7.15 shows the rectified output across a 1 kΩ load resistor.

Fig. 7.16 shows the Pspice schematic for an unregulated supply, which adds an output capacitor in parallel with the load resistor. The value of the capacitor was chosen for this example to give a noticeable ripple. Fig. 7.17 shows the unregulated output.

Fig. 7.18 shows the regulated power supply. This circuit uses a Zener diode as the voltage reference; its breakdown voltage is 5.1 V. The resistor feeding the Zener diode is chosen to give a 20 mA current. The $R1, R3$ voltage divider is designed to divide the desired output voltage of 10 V to a level equal to the Zener reference voltage; their series resistance is chosen to be a high value to minimize their current draw on the power supply output. Fig. 7.19 shows that the

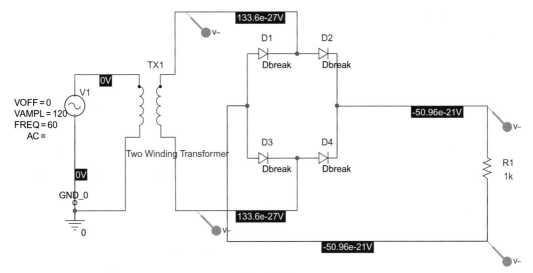

Fig. 7.14
Simulation schematic for a full-wave rectifier circuit.

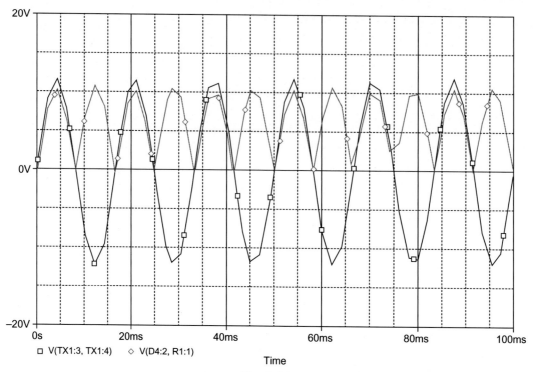

Fig. 7.15
Output of the full-wave rectifier circuit.

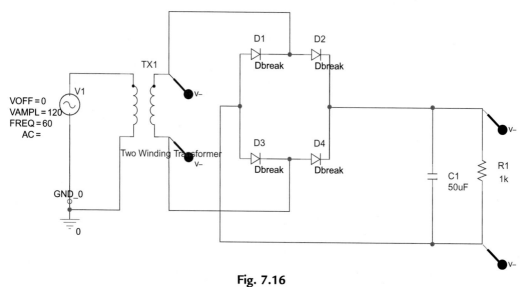

Fig. 7.16
Simulation schematic for an unregulated power supply.

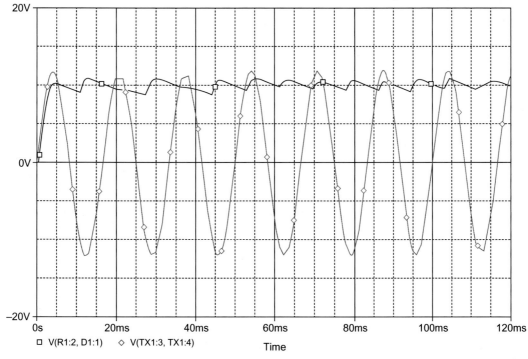

Fig. 7.17

Output of the unregulated power supply.

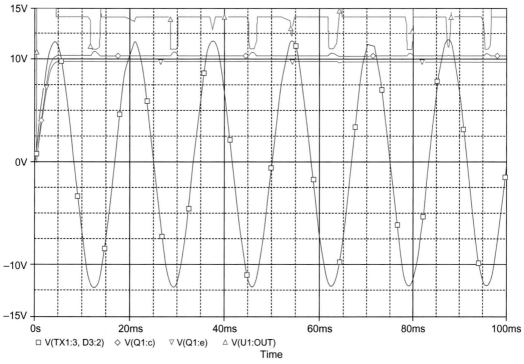

Fig. 7.18

Simulation schematic for a regulated power supply.

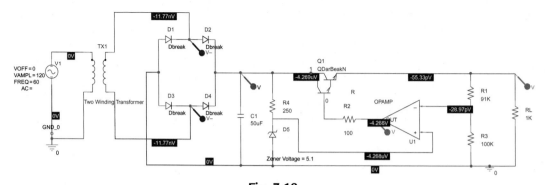

Fig. 7.19
Output of the regulated power supply.

regulated output is very smooth without the need for an additional capacitor across the load. The plot also shows the op amp output that controls the regulator transistor.

7.7 Thermal Characteristics and Heat Dissipation

We need to control the temperature of electronics for several reasons: circuit characteristics may vary significantly over wide temperature ranges, high temperatures cause components to fail more rapidly, and very high temperatures may pose a fire hazard.

A critical thermal parameter for semiconductors is **maximum junction temperature** $T_{j,\ max}$. Junction temperature refers to the semiconductor junctions; if these junctions go above a specified temperature, either the device quickly destroys itself or its thermal protection circuits shut down the device. A value of $T_{j,\ max} = 150°$C is common for digital VLSI while power semiconductors may see ratings of $T_{j,\ max} = 85°$C. We maintain all the semiconductors below $T_{j,\ max}$ using a combination of low-power design to reduce the heat generated and heat dissipation to efficiently remove heat from the devices.

The TO-220 **heat sink**, shown in Fig. 7.20 , is designed to be mechanically compatible with the TO-220 package, used by a number of electronic components. The component can be bolted onto the heat sink. The thermal connection to the heat sink allows for improved heat dissipation.

Fan *vs.* fanless design is an important design decision in many systems. Fans greatly improve cooling but introduce acoustic noise. If fans are used to reduce component temperatures, the enclosure must be properly designed to allow for airflow into and out of the cooling region.

We can analyze the temperature of components using a **thermal resistance** model [74]. In this model, thermal resistance is analogous to electrical resistance, heat is analogous to current, and

Fig. 7.20
A TO-220 heat sink and device.

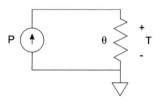

Fig. 7.21
A circuit model for thermal dissipation.

temperature is analogous to voltage. The **ambient temperature**—the temperature of the surroundings—can be treated as analogous to electrical ground if the circuit cannot generate enough heat to substantially increase the ambient temperature.

Many components are rated with a thermal resistance by manufacturers. When a component is connected to a heat sink, the system has a lower thermal resistance. We can also use various thermal compounds between the component and the heat sink to reduce the thermal resistance from the core device to the ambient.

Fig. 7.21 shows the circuit model for a simple thermal dissipation problem: the component dissipates power P and has a thermal resistance θ to the ambient. The ambient is shown as a ground but it has a nonzero reference value T_A. The temperature difference T from the component temperature T_C to the ambient T_A is

$$T_C = T_A + P\theta. \tag{7.15}$$

Our goal for semiconductor cooling is to ensure that $T_C < T_{j, max}$.

When a device is not mounted on a heat sink, we use the junction-ambient thermal resistance θ_{JA}. This value is given by the manufacturer in many cases.[1] In the case of the LM340 voltage regulator in a TO-220 package, $\theta_{JA} = 54°C/W$ [40]. At a power dissipation of 5 W and an ambient temperature of $25°C$, the LM340's junction temperature is $295°C$, clearly too high.

When we connect the device to a heat sink, we just compute the thermal resistance of the assembly [3]:

$$\theta_{JA} = \theta_{JC} + \theta_{CS} + \theta_{SA} \tag{7.16}$$

where θ_{JC} is the junction-to-case thermal resistance, θ_{CS} is the case-to-heat sink thermal resistance determined by the thermal paste applied between the device and heat sink, and θ_{SA} is the heat sink-to-ambient thermal resistance. In the case of the LM340 and TO-220 package, $\theta_{JC} = 4°C/W$. We can use a typical value of $\theta_{CS} = 0.1°C/W$. The TO-220 heat sink data sheet quotes $\theta_{SA} = 12°C/W$ for no airflow [30]. This gives $\theta_{JA} = 16.1°C/W$ and $T_J = 105.5°C$, well within the safe zone for this device.

Active cooling using fans makes a big difference in junction temperatures. If we provide an airflow of 5m/s, $\theta_{SA} = 4°C/W$ and $T_J = 65.5°C$.

Heat causes electrical and electronic components to age and fail faster. Aging mechanisms can be traced back to chemical and physical processes. The **Arrhenius equation** describes the relationship between the rate of a physical mechanism and temperature [52]; it has been shown to apply to a wide variety of processes related to aging. The equation has the form

$$r = Ae^{-E_a/kT} \tag{7.17}$$

where r is the rate of the process, A is the **Arrhenius prefactor** for a given physical mechanism, and E_a is the **activation energy**. The exponential dependence of rate on temperature means that rate doubles for a $10°C$ temperature rise.

The aging of electrolytic capacitors is an example of the application of the Arrhenius equation [49]. The lifetime of an electrolytic capacitor as a function of operating and ambient temperature is

$$L = L_0 2^{(T_{max} - T_a)/10} \tag{7.18}$$

where L_0 is the capacitor's specified lifetime, T_{max} is the maximum temperature, and T_a is the ambient temperature.

---

[1] They do not always make finding those values easy, however. The LM340 datasheet from National Semiconductor relegated the thermal resistance values to a footnote.

Aluminum electrolytic capacitor has higher losses than do some types of capacitors. As a result, ripple currents generate heat. The ripple current at an arbitrary frequency is referenced to a standard frequency by the formula

$$I = \frac{I_x}{k} \qquad (7.19)$$

where I_x is the actual ripple frequency and k is a coefficient specified for the part. The increase in temperature at the surface of the capacitor caused by ripple current is

$$\triangle T_c = \frac{I^2 R}{\beta S} \qquad (7.20)$$

where I is the ripple current, R is the equivalent series resistance of the capacitor, and S is the capacitor's surface area, and

$$\beta = 2.3 \times 10^{-3} \cdot S^{-0.2}. \qquad (7.21)$$

The temperature increase at the capacitor's core is

$$\triangle T_j = \triangle T_s \left(\frac{I}{I_0}\right)^2 \qquad (7.22)$$

where I_0 is the rated ripple current of the capacitor.

7.8 Power Management

Most computer systems make use of power management implemented through a combination of hardware and software. The system may turn off units that are not currently in use; it may also run some units at lower voltages and clock speeds to conserve power.

An interface may need to accept power management signals and shut off some circuits. Power-up is often the trickiest part of power management. Any state that was held in dynamic devices must be restored from a nonvolatile memory; in some cases it can be recomputed by running the system. Analog circuits may display transients as the circuits power up or down—the click of an audio system during power up/down or when headphones are connected or disconnected are a classic example of annoying transients.

Further Reading

Sauvageau [50] describes testing procedures for USB power adapters and the design characteristics that affect both power performance and safety. *Battery Reference Book* [15] describes a broad range of battery chemistries.

Questions

Q7.1   You are given this diode bridge with a sinusoidal input:

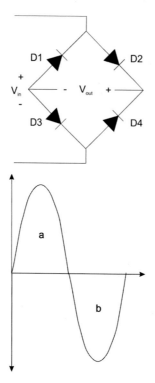

(a)   Which diodes are on in region *a*?
(b)   Which diodes are on in region *b*?

Q7.2   A 12 V, 60 Hz power supply includes an output-stage capacitor of 50 μF. What is the maximum allowable load current to keep the ripple within 2%?

Q7.3   Draw the waveforms for the operation of a buck converter, including the switch, V_C, and I_L.

Q7.4   Draw the waveforms for the operation of a boost converter, including the switch, V_C, and I_L.

Q7.5   An IC dissipates 10 W and has a maximum junction temperature $T_{j,\ max} = 150°$C. The ambient temperature is 20°C.

If the device is exposed directly to the ambient without a heat sink, what is the required thermal resistance of the package to keep the device's junction temperature below the specified maximum?

What must the package's thermal resistance if it is used with a heat sink with thermal resistance $\theta_{SA} = 12°$C/W and $\theta_{CS} = 0.1°$C/W?

CHAPTER 8

Interface Design

8.1 Introduction

We now have a toolbox of techniques, both analog and digital, for interface design. It is time to put these techniques together to design complete interfaces. The interface is itself a part of a larger embedded system and the interface design process is one part of the overall embedded system design.

The design of an embedded system interface can be seen as the placement of two boundaries:

- The boundary between the software on the CPU and the interface's digital hardware.
- The boundary between the interface's digital hardware and its analog hardware.

Section 8.2 develops characteristics of common use cases for embedded devices. Section 8.3 looks at requirements on interfaces. Section 8.4 introduces the architecture of an embedded system interface. Section 8.5 considers how to choose a good computing platform. Fig. 8.6 discusses circuit construction technologies. Section 8.7 considers closed-loop control systems. Section 8.8 examines the hardware/software boundary. Section 8.9 develops a simple driver. Section 8.10 looks at the digital/analog boundary. Section 8.11 puts together these concepts as part of the interface design methodology. We then develop two examples: a clap detector in Section 8.12 and a simple motor controller in Section 8.13.

8.2 Embedded System Use Cases

Understanding the characteristics of use cases for embedded systems helps us to identify the important characteristics of their interfaces.

We can infer some basic requirements on the processor and interfaces based on characteristics of the application:

- *CPU performance* is a key driver of software development; the class of CPU required to meet performance requirements also constraints the available microcontroller or system-on-chip platforms and their associated interfaces.

Embedded System Interfacing. https://doi.org/10.1016/B978-0-12-817402-9.00008-X

Table 8.1 System requirements for common embedded use cases.

Requirements	Audio-Rate Signal Processing	Closed-Loop Control	Event Processing
CPU performance	High	Medium to high	Low
Sample rate	High	Medium to high	Low
Network bandwidth	Medium	Low	Low

- *Sample rate* is related to the software load but also to the performance requirements on the interfaces.
- *Network bandwidth requirements* to the outside world may constrain the interconnection bandwidth available within the embedded platform.

Table 8.1 estimates these requirements for several common embedded applications: audio-rate signal processing, in the range of several kilohertz, could be applied to applications other than audio; closed-loop control uses a microcontroller to provide commands to a machine to perform in a specified manner; event processing generates data when a specified change in the environment is registered.

8.3 Interface Specifications

We can identify two types of specifications on interfaces: requirements on the interface characteristics and properties of the design process.

Given that interfaces process signals, we are certainly interested in the requirements on that signal processing as determined by the application. Signal processing requirements may relate to both time and resolution.

The **data rate** or **sample rate** limits the frequency characteristics of our signal. The **latency** of processing is often critical; analog/digital and hardware/software design choices may be determined by how long we have to process a signal.

The **precision** and **dynamic range** of a signal reflect the required resolution of the signal. Interface design needs to preserve enough dynamic range of the signal to allow the required processing to be completed.

Power consumption is a key parameter for many designs. Battery-operated devices should be designed to maximize battery life. High power consumption may also lead to excessive heat dissipation.

The design process must consider both the **manufacturing cost** and the **design time** of the interface. Both are important and the two may be at odds with each other. The cost of the interface depends on the components selected as well as the costs of fabricating the associated circuit board. Design time is itself a cost; design time may also delay deployment of the product.

Interfaces that are simpler to design may increase manufacturing cost; they could also increase the development cost of the system software. Conversely, a more sophisticated design that requires greater design effort may lower manufacturing costs.

8.4 Interface Architecture

Fig. 8.1 shows an architecture template that describes a wide range of interfaces. The bus connects to data and status registers that provide the software interface to the application. A **mode FSM** controls the operation of the interface. Digital and analog subsystems perform processing on plant signals from the physical world. User controls provide users with means to control the interface separate from the CPU.

The interface registers provide the only visible state shared by the microcontroller and the interface device. Any software control of the interface must be done by manipulating the registers. We can typically divide interface registers into *mode* and *data* categories, with mode registers controlling operation while data registers provide the values. Some registers may be read-only while others will be read/write.

The interface operation can be viewed as a finite-state machine. The mode FSM may be an explicit state machine implemented as logic and registers; it may also be implicit in the operation of the interface circuits. The interface goes into modes based on its own activity; the microcontroller checks status, manipulates data, and may change the mode register to cause the interface FSM to change state. A very simple interface FSM is shown in Fig. 8.2. The *idle* state may occur when the device has completed an operation. By changing the mode

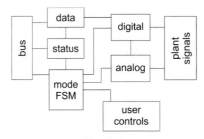

Fig. 8.1
Architecture template for interfaces.

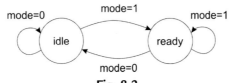

Fig. 8.2
A simple interface mode FSM.

register, the microcontroller can signal the interface to move to the *ready* state and perform another operation.

8.5 Choosing the Right Platform

The interface designer doesn't always have the ability to choose the computing platform on the other side of the interface. We sometimes have to live with the characteristics of a microcontroller or SoC which was chosen for reasons beyond the characteristics of the embedded interface. No matter who chooses the platform, its characteristics shape the design of the interface.

The **hardware platform** includes several related components:

*   The processor or, in the case of high-performance systems, several processors. Some of the processors may provide only limited programmability, as is the case for many video accelerators.
*   The set of I/O devices provided by the platform.
*   The bus interface.
*   The software development environment.

The **software platform** includes:

*   A hardware abstraction layer (HAL), board support package (BSP), or basic input/output system (BIOS).
*   Device drivers.
*   An executive or operating system.

If our platform is built from several chips, we may be able to separate these choices to some degree. However, modern platforms often take the form of a single-chip microcontroller or system-on-chip. In these cases, the platform selection process must balance these potentially competing factors.

CPU performance determines what part of the system functionality can be put in software. CPU performance may enforce absolute limits—it may not run fast enough to perform, for example, digital filtering operations. But performance can also be evaluated relative to the rest of the application. A system with a large software load may leave few cycles for interface-oriented operations, no matter how much performance it provides.

We should keep in mind that CPU performance depends on a number of factors. There is no one best choice for a CPU instruction set or microarchitecture. A CPU that works well for one workload may perform poorly for another workload. CPU performance should be evaluated not on the basis of generic workloads but by using workloads that reflect the characteristics of the target application.

CPU utilization is a key metric for real-time embedded systems. Utilization is defined as the fractional amount of CPU execution time of a set of tasks C_i over a given interval T:

$$U = \frac{1}{T}\sum_i C_i. \qquad (8.1)$$

We often express utilization as a percentage. Utilization may vary over the course of operation as the workload varies. We are generally interested in worst-case utilization over any interval. We cannot exceed 100% utilization that would require more CPU time than is available. The maximum available utilization of the CPU depends in part on the real-time scheduling algorithm used.

Interrupt latency is a critical design parameter for high-speed I/O processing. CPUs themselves can introduce dozens of clock cycles of processing time into the interrupt; the interrupt driver itself adds more overhead as it saves and restores registers.

The **arithmetic precision** required for I/O processing is affected by the choice of CPU. We can always combine smaller words to perform wider integer operations or to perform floating-point operations in software, but software-implemented extended arithmetic requires additional CPU time.

The platform comes with some set of **I/O devices and interfaces**. Any devices or interfaces that are required for the project but not part of the basic platform must be designed into the interface. Relatively few modern chips directly expose the CPU bus. General-purpose I/O (GPIO) pins are a common form of interface; these pins are easy to use but provide only modest speeds. Some chips may provide an external DRAM interface that could also be used for other devices; such interfaces are much faster but also much more challenging design targets.

Bus performance of the I/O system. The bus throughput is proportional to the product of bus width and bus clock cycle time. CPU busses come at many different design points providing different cost/performance trade-offs. While high-performance busses provide faster I/O, they also require more complex interface designs for the peripherals attached to them.

The **software development environment** (**SDE**) will influence the overall development process. Not only do the features of the SDE determine how code will be developed, but its debugging capabilities will influence how much of the interface debugging can be accomplished from the software side *vs.* using test instruments such as logic analyzers. An **integrated development environment** (**IDE**) provides a graphical user interface for the tools in the software development environment.

On the software side of the platform, we can identify several basic components, some of which may be supplied with the CPU or board while others may be acquired separately. Most systems use low-level routines to provide basic functions: boot, real time clock, etc. This low-level software can be called any of several names: hardware abstraction layer, board support package, or BIOS (a term from the IBM Personal Computer).

Fig. 8.3 shows a **layer diagram** for the software organization of the embedded system. The hardware platform is at the bottom layer. The hardware abstraction layer provides basic software functions. Drivers may work through HAL functions or directly on the software. The executive or operating system controls the operations of tasks that perform the application-level functions.

While the hardware abstraction layer may provide some drivers for standard functions such as USB, the designer may need to provide other drivers. A driver for the interface must be designed. The details of driver design depend on the type of operating system or executive used. We will discuss driver design in more detail in Sections 8.8 and 8.9.

The term **executive** is an early term for a simple operating system. A **real-time operating system** is designed specifically to provide real-time responsiveness for both I/O and process execution. Linux is widely used in embedded devices; not all versions of Linux are designed to provide highly responsive performance for I/O and real-time operation.

We will refer to the top-level software units as **tasks,** each of which is a single thread of execution that is guaranteed to terminate in a finite amount of time. A task may run more than once, either sporadically or periodically. A complete application may be composed of several tasks.

A system with a small number of tasks may use interrupts to manage task execution. Periodic tasks can be controlled by a timer. Sporadic events can also be used to trigger interrupts. Given that microprocessors have a limited number of interrupt lines, this approach does not scale to large number of tasks.

A **cyclic executive** [6] can be used to provide predictable timing behavior for periodic tasks in a simple real-time system. If each task has its own period, the pattern of task activations is

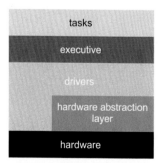

Fig. 8.3
Layer diagram for the embedded system.

equal in length to the least-common multiple—also known as the **hyperperiod**—of the task periods. The hyperperiod defines a **major cycle** for the operation of the executive. The **schedule** is the order of execution of the tasks in the major cycle. The **minor cycle** must be at least as small as the shortest period of any task. The executive is called or enabled once per minor cycle by an interrupt. It keeps track of its progress through the major cycle to control what tasks are performed.

Fig. 8.4 gives pseudo-code for a simple cyclic executive. The executive is contained inside a while (TRUE) loop. The timer interrupt causes its handler timer_ISR() to set a flag minor_cycle_flag that is visible by the main routine and to update a counter minor_cycle_count that gives the value of the current minor cycle. The executive proceeds only when the flag is set, indicating that another minor cycle has been completed; it resets the flag to prepare for the next minor cycle. It then uses a counter to determine which part of the major cycle should be executed next. A task is implemented as a function. Each task must terminate in a finite amount of time. Once the function returns, the executive returns to wait for the next minor cycle to finish.

A **real-time operating system (RTOS)** uses preemptive multitasking. A timer is used to call the operating system once per **time quantum**. At each time quantum, the current state of the executing task is saved; the RTOS determines what thread should run next; it then restores the state of the selected task. RTOSs typically support a **priority-driven** scheduling policy—the highest-priority ready task runs.

```
int minor_cycle_count = 0, /* counter for minor cycle */
    minor_cycle_flag = 0; /* barrier flag for minor cycle */

void timer_ISR() { /* respond to timer interrupt */
    minor_cycle_flag = 1; /* lower barrier flag */
    /* update count, roll over if necessary */
    if (++minor_cycle_count == HYPERPERIOD) minor_cycle_count = 0;
}

void main() {
    while (TRUE) {
        while (!minor_cycle_flag); /* wait for timer interrupt */
        minor_cycle_flag = 0; /* reset flag */
        switch (minor_cycle_count) {
            case 0: major_0(); break;
            case 1: major_1(); break;
            /* … continue for remainder of major cycle */
            default: executive _error();
        }
    }
}
```

Fig. 8.4

A cyclic executive.

8.6 Construction Technologies

Some electronics construction technologies are designed for one-off prototyping; others were created to manufacture multiple units.

Fig. 8.5 shows a radio manufactured by the Atwater Kent Manufacturing Company in Philadelphia in the early 1920s. Thanks to the opening of KDKA in Pittsburgh and the birth of commercial radio broadcasting, radios changed in a matter of months from esoteric experimental equipment to a centerpiece for homes of the well-to-do. Atwater Kent made several radio models built on boards such as this one. These radios came to be known as **breadboards** after the boards used to cut bread in kitchens of the day. The company advertised the breadboard construction as a means to display the high quality of their components; it is equally likely that the style was dictated by the breathtaking speed with which the radio market expanded. *Breadboard* later came to mean a prototype circuit built on a board with point-to-point hand wiring even though the original term referred to an expensive manufactured device.

The prototyping module of Fig. 1.16 allows easy construction of certain classes of circuits, namely, dual inline packages and components with extended leads. Protoboards cannot connect to surface mount devices without adapters. Protoboards are prone to large parasitic values due both to loose wiring and the connections themselves.

Early printed circuit board manufacturing relied on **through-hole** connections between a component and the board. As shown in Fig. 8.6, a hole was drilled through the PCB and plated with copper. The component lead was inserted in the hole, which was then filled with solder. Modern PCBs primarily use **surface mount** connections that solder the lead to a copper pad on the surface of the board. Some chips provide **solder bump** connections in an array across the bottom of the chip.

Fig. 8.5
An Atwater Kent breadboard radio.

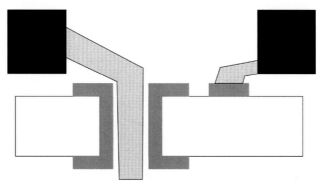

Fig. 8.6
Through-hole and surface-mount connections on a printed circuit board.

8.7 *Control and Closed-Loop Systems*

Feedback control is a fundamental engineering technique for controlling all sorts of **physical plants**: mechanical, electrical, chemical. The feedback controller generates an error signal as the difference between the actual output of the plant and the desired output. The **control law** defines the controller response which commands the plant to change its state closer to produce an output closer to the desired value. A block diagram for a feedback control system is shown in Fig. 8.7. The **command** is $X(t)$ in the continuous time case or $x(n)$ in the discrete time case; the error signal is $E(t)$ or $e(n)$; the controller output is $K(t)$ or $k(n)$; the system response is $Y(t)$ or $y(n)$.

We typically specify the control system based on its step response, which represents its response to an instantaneous change in the command. Three characteristics are used to describe the step response:

- **Rise time** is the time from the command to the first time at which the response reaches a specified value, typically 90% of the asymptotic response.
- **Overshoot** is the maximum value of the response.
- **Settling time** is the time at which the response is bounded within some amount of the asymptotic response, with $\pm 1\%$ a typical value.

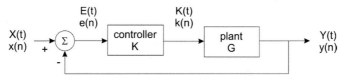

Fig. 8.7
Block diagram of a feedback controller.

A classical approach models both the plant and controller as linear systems. A typical second-order transfer function for a physical plant is

$$G(s) = \frac{1}{as^2 + bs + c}.$$ (8.2)

If the controller response is $K(s)$, the closed-loop transfer function is

$$H(s) = \frac{K(s)G(s)}{1 + K(s)G(s)}.$$ (8.3)

A **proportional-integral-derivative (PID)** control law [22] provides a blend of desirable characteristics and is widely used. As the name implies, this control law includes proportional, integral, and derivative terms, each with its own weight. The proportional component provides the basic response to a command input. The integral component ensures that the controller has zero asymptotic error. The derivative component can be tuned to provide fast response to new commands.

Here is the continuous version of a PID control law:

$$K(t) = K_p E(t) + K_i \int_0^t E(t)dt + K_d \frac{dE(t)}{dt}.$$ (8.4)

The **controller gains** K_p, K_i, K_d determine the relative weight given to each component of the control law. The continuous form can be translated to a discrete form:

$$k(n) = K_p e(n) + K_i \sum_{0 \leq k \leq n} e(k) + K_d[e(n) - e(n-1)].$$ (8.5)

A modified form differentiates on the control output y rather than the error signal e to avoid a sharp change in the command producing a large derivative term in the control law:

$$k(n) = K_p e(n) + K_i \sum_{0 \leq k \leq n} e(k) + K_d[y(n) - y(n-1)].$$ (8.6)

A PID controller is a second-order system:

$$K_{PID}(s) = K_p + \frac{K_i}{s} + K_d s.$$ (8.7)

Its response can take the form of the sum of two exponentials or of a damped sinusoid.

The response of the closed-loop system depends on the plant. For example, consider a first-order plant:

$$G(s) = \frac{1}{(s + p_1)}.$$ (8.8)

This plant has an exponential response which only asymptotically approaches a final value. When we wrap a PID controller around the plant, the system response becomes

$$H(s) = \frac{K_d s^2 + K_p s + K_i}{s(s + p_1) + K_d s^2 + K_p s + K_i}.$$

(8.9)

The PID-controlled system has a second-order response which, with proper tuning of the controller gains, can provide a much more responsive system.

In theory, we should know the parameters of the plant transfer function, from which we can determine the controller gains based on the rise and settling times. In practice, we do not always know the plant parameters. In that case, we can experiment with the system to empirically determine the controller gains.

Complex control systems may change their response depending on some condition: user input, changes to the load presented, etc. **Hybrid control** specifies modes as states that can specify parameters for the controller. Hybrid control design checks that the system response at mode changes meets characteristics such as smoothness.

We need to choose a sample rate for a digital controller. We want the control sample rate to be considerably higher than the highest frequency pole of the control transfer function.

8.8 The Hardware/Software Boundary

The partition between software running on the CPU and interface hardware is the basic decision in interface design. We can expand on our requirements to identify several factors that influence the decision.

Algorithmic complexity. Some algorithms may be hard to implement as analog or digital circuits due to their size or the nature of the operations they perform.

Flexibility. Flexibility comes in several forms. A software routine may be changed after installation of the system. The software may also provide parameters that adjust its operation without changing the code itself. Updates are definitely easier for software than for hardware interfaces. The more parameters for a given function, the more expensive and difficult is the application of those parameters to a hardware implementation.

CPU utilization. An interface can be used to offload some processing from the CPU. High data rates are particularly taxing for software. The cost of a faster CPU must be balanced against the cost of a more sophisticated hardware interface.

Sample rate. CPUs have some basic limits on the rate at which they can process data. Interrupt handling, RTOS overhead, and software performance all limit the speed with which the

CPU can perform a computation. An interface can be used to recognize events or to downsample the signals.

Numerical precision and dynamic range. The range between minimum and maximum values on a signal determines both the number of bits required to represent the signal as well as whether that representation is fixed point or floating point. While floating-point units can be built in hardware, such designs are relatively complex. Number representations with larger bit widths increase the size of hardware data paths. In contrast, software number representations may take up more memory but CPU mechanisms exist for several different number representations of varying accuracy.

Latency. Software processing adds latency for interrupt processing and RTOS mechanisms; individual operations may require multiple instructions. Digital interfaces may provide low latency and analog interfaces can be highly responsive.

Many devices will make use of the microcontroller's interrupt interface. The interrupt system allows devices to change the flow of execution in the CPU to an **interrupt handler**, also known as the **interrupt service routine** (**ISR**). Operations in the ISR are performed at the hardware priority level defined by the interrupt—the operating system has no control over those priorities. Hardware interrupts will block other software tasks, including the operating system. As a result, the real-time properties of the system may be violated. The ISR should perform the minimum operations required to service the interrupt; other tasks can be performed in a software task that is under control of the operating system.

As shown in Fig. 8.8, several different software objects are involved in the processing flow of data as it moves from input to output. Interrupt service routines handle the input and output tasks themselves. A software task performs processing. The data flowing into the task goes through one buffer while another buffer handles the flow of data out of the task. Fig. 8.9 shows a UML sequence diagram for the flow of data.

Fig. 8.10 shows a UML state diagram for a driver. Upon entry, the driver typically checks the status of the device to understand what type of service needs to be performed. It may

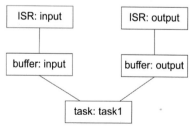

Fig. 8.8
UML object diagram for data handling objects.

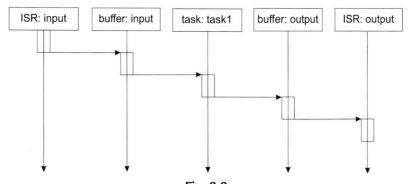

Fig. 8.9
UML sequence diagram for data handling flow.

Fig. 8.10
A UML state diagram for a driver.

manipulate data, either reading or writing. It then updates the status of the device, for example, to enable its next operation.

8.9 Example: A Simple Driver

We can better understand driver design through a simple character string output interface. While the device itself is of limited practical use, it illustrates basic concepts in drivers without unnecessary complexity. The device is used to output a string of characters, one character at a time.

Fig. 8.11 shows a block diagram for the character interface. The device includes three registers, two one-bit and one eight-bit. The character task writes a character into the *char* register,

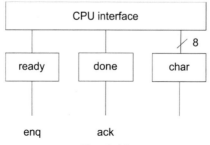

Fig. 8.11
Block diagram of a simple character output interface.

then sets *ready* to 1. The external system sets *ack* to 1 when it has processed the character. The *ack* register's output is connected directly to the interrupt logic while *ready* and *char* are connected to address logic that maps them into the CPU memory space.

Fig. 8.12 shows the state transition diagram for the mode FSM. The device is normally at idle. When activated by *ready*, it starts to output the current character. It enters the *done* state when it receives an acknowledgment. When the task resets the *done* bit, the interface returns to the *idle* state. This design is an example of an implicit mode FSM. The interface states are defined by combinations of the status bits; state transitions are caused in this case entirely by external inputs with no additional logic. Table 8.2 presents the mapping of status bits to state names; the code 01 is not used.

This design could be extended to use DMA—the DMA controller would interact directly with the hardware to output the character string. The device state machine may need to be adjusted to be compatible with the DMA protocol. Given that DMA imposes regular timing on the character stream, the other side of the interface may drop some characters.

Figs. 8.13 and 8.14 show the character output task and the interface driver, respectively. Fig. 8.15 gives a UML sequence diagram for an output sequence. The task starts a character output by loading the character and setting *ready*. When the interface receives an *ack* signal, it raises an interrupt that activates the driver. The driver, in turn, sets char_done_flag to tell the task that the character output is complete.

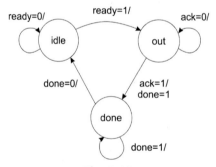

Fig. 8.12
Mode FSM for the character output interface.

Table 8.2 State encoding for the character output interface FSM

State	Code (Ready, Done)
idle	00
out	10
done	11

```
void char_string() {
      pos = 0;
      while (pos < MAXPOS) { /* stop at end of string */
            poke(CHAR_CHAR,string[pos++]);
                  /* set next character, update index */
            poke(CHAR_READY, 1); /* start the device */
            while (!char_done_flag); /* wait for character to finish */
            char_done_flag = 0;
      }
}
```

Fig. 8.13
The character string writing task.

```
void char_driver() {
      if (!peek(CHAR_DONE)) error(); /* sanity check */
      poke(CHAR_READY, 0); /* reset ready */
      char_done_flag = 1;
}
```

Fig. 8.14
The character output driver.

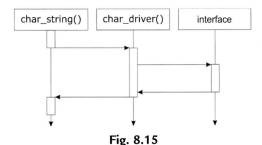

Fig. 8.15
UML sequence diagram for operation of the character output interface.

8.10 The Analog/Digital Boundary

The analog/digital boundary within the interface determines some important characteristics of the interface. Of course, some signals present themselves as analog. However, we often have some choice as to how much processing to perform on the signals in analog form before converting them to digital form.

Signal characteristics. Some signals may be electrically unsuitable for digital logic. Either very small or very large voltages or currents may require conditioning before being handed off to digital logic.

Dynamic range. Processing on a signal may affect its dynamic range.

Temperature sensitivity. Analog circuits are more sensitive to temperature. Component values vary with temperature, resulting in varying circuit characteristics. While analog circuits can be designed to be resistant to temperature variations, digital logic is much more tolerant of temperature variation.

Power consumption. Analog circuits often consume less power to perform a given function than is the case for an equivalent digital logic circuit.

Cost. Some important operations can be performed by very simple analog circuits with a very small number of components. The equivalent digital design may be more expensive.

Latency. The small number of components in an analog circuit often translates to very low latency.

8.11 Interface Design Methodologies

Interface design is one phase of embedded system design. As with any subsystem, we want to separate its detailed design from the rest of the system to the extent possible. But we need to inform the interface design process from the system design: requirements, specification, architecture, and testing.

System requirements and specification include requirements on the signals that will be processed by the interface:

* Input and output signals.
* Analog *vs.* digital values.
* For analog signals, signal levels and dynamic range.
* For digital values, logic levels and timing parameters.

Requirements and specification also capture the processing to be performed on those signals:

* Sample rate.
* Algorithm.
* Latency.

The requirements phase also captures the economic factors of design effort and manufacturing cost.

Based on these requirements, the architecture phase sets the software/hardware boundary. This **design partitioning** process determines what part of the processing will be performed in the CPU versus the interface. This hardware/software boundary is determined in part by technical factors such as sample rate and algorithmic complexity. These factors define a design space which describes the set of feasible designs. Economic factors further constrain the feasible design space.

Fig. 8.16 illustrates a decision process for design partitioning. The sample rate for the signal is a key factor in determining what can be done using software on the CPU versus what needs to be

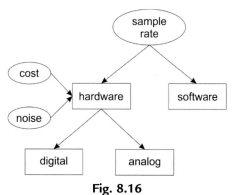

Fig. 8.16
Interface design partitioning process.

done in the interface hardware. Once we have decided what part of the system will reside in hardware, component cost and noise are two important factors that help to determine what functions should be built with digital logic or analog circuits.

Component selection is a critical part of the design process. While some components can be selected later, the selection of major components is part of the architecture phase—the characteristics of some analog and digital components will shape the design of the rest of the interface. Components are selected from catalogs, usually online but occasionally on paper. A catalog may come from a manufacturer and describe the range of components they make. A catalog may also come from a supplier who carries the products of several manufacturers. Search tools are a valuable aid in narrowing down the set of possible components. Many Web sites allow you to enter one or more specifications that are used to narrow the search. Typically entering a few parameters narrows the set of components down to a handful. If a given search results in no results, you need to rethink those parameters and find a set value that is inhabited by a suitable component. Schematic capture tools also provide databases of components and their parameters; these databases allow you to experiment with components before you order.

At this point, design on the interface can proceed relatively independently. Some aspects of the design may be performed relatively independently of the processor platform. Analog design can proceed using a combination of simulators and breadboard circuits. Digital computation units can be designed using standard HDL techniques. However, design of the processor interface may require a prototype. Manufacturers do not often provide HDL models for the CPU bus interface. While a model can be constructed as part of the design process, running the interface against a working bus helps to build confidence in the design.

Interface testing introduces several complexities beyond software testing. First, as we just saw, we may not have an executable or simulatable model of the CPU bus interface. The only way to test the bus interface may be to plug it into the system; this step will also require software scaffolding. Second, analog test signals cannot be captured as data files, as can digital test sequences. Documentation should carefully describe the analog test setup: what signals are generated, the equipment used to generate those signals, and the tests performed on the analog circuits to verify their behavior.

8.12 Example: Clap Detector

A **clap detector** is a good example of filtering and detection. We can design the clap detector with any of several different hardware/software partitions. We can build a clap detector entirely using analog circuits. However, a purely analog detector would be hard to adjust for clap detection parameters. We may want to adjust level based on the audio environment. The transition and duration may need to be adjusted depending on the amount of echo.

As shown in Fig. 8.17, a clap produces an audio signal in the classic form of a damped exponential. The clap's large damping results in its sharp sound. This waveform suggests a detector architecture that allows us to substantially reduce the CPU's sampling rate. We are not concerned with all the details of the audio signal—the envelope of the clap is sufficient. We can use an envelope detector similar to those we saw in Section 5.13 to rectify and filter the waveform. A low-pass op amp filter can provide a signal to the ADC that is substantially smoother than the original audio filter. We can use a software correlator to compare the input waveform to an exponential model to detect the waveform.

Fig. 8.18 shows the block diagram of the clap detector: envelope detection rectifies and filters the input signal; the ADC generates samples; the detector compares the sampled waveform to a model of the clap exponential. The low-pass filter allows us to operate the analog/digital converter at a lower sample rate than would be required for full audio intelligibility. Reducing

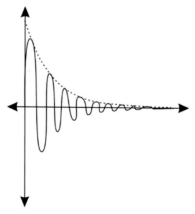

Fig. 8.17
A clap waveform and its envelope.

Fig. 8.18
Block diagram of a clap detector.

the sample rate reduces both the CPU utilization and the sizes of buffers required for the condition operations.

8.13 Example: Motor Controller

Motor control circuits add capabilities and greater precision. We can use feedback to control the speed of the motor—rather than just providing a given amount of power and assuming that it runs at the desired rate, we can measure the speed of the motor and adjust its drive to maintain the speed we want. We can go one step further to build a motor that stops at a commanded position and can be turned to a new position at will.

DC motors come in any of several different designs:

- A **brushed DC motor** is the old-fashioned style of motor with commutator brushes that provide alternating connections to the motor windings to keep the motor spinning.
- A **brushless DC motor** does not have commutator brushes. Instead, it uses a controller to switch the connections to the motor windings.
- A **servo motor** is designed to stop at various positions.
- A **stepper motor** has more poles than does a servo motor, providing finer control.

The torque produced by a motor is proportional to its current [10]:

$$T = K_t I. \tag{8.10}$$

The movement of the motor coils induces a **back electromotive force** or **back EMF** that counters the voltage applied to the motor. The back EMF V_e depends on the rotation speed or angular velocity of the motor shaft:

$$V_e = K_e \dot{\theta}. \tag{8.11}$$

A motor has several specifications, some of which are independent of the control. The operating voltage, maximum current, and maximum rotating speed of the motor are all characteristics that depend on the motor design and are independent of the control we apply to it. The motor characteristics need to be matched to the requirements of the mechanism that the motor will drive.

Selecting a motor is a simple example of the use of online catalogs. A variety of sites allow users to first select DC motors as a category, then specify several search filters: speed,

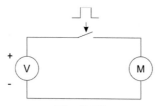

Fig. 8.19
Pulse-width modulation determination of motor speed.

torque, voltage, etc. Our example design will use a motor [43] that operates at 0.23 W at 6 V; at its maximum efficiency point it spins at 2089 RPM.

As shown in Fig. 8.19, we use **pulse-width modulation** to vary the speed of a motor; we can apply this technique to both brushed and brushless motors. If we applied the power supply voltage continuously, the motor would run at some maximum speed. As we reduce the duty cycle D of the power supply, the motor coasts during the off interval. The result is an average speed which depends linearly on the power supply duty cycle. We can reverse the rotational direction of the motor by reversing the polarity of the power supply relative to the motor's terminals.

The duty cycle resolution is the minimum allowable change to the duty cycle. This resolution determines the precision with which we can adjust the motor speed.

The PWM function is often implemented as a hardware block. Performing the PWM function entirely in software would require a responsive CPU to keep up with time ticks. As shown in Fig. 8.20, a PWM unit consists of a timer and a comparator. The timer counts clock pulses; its period determines the PWM period. A separate register holds a *compare* value that determines when the PWM output switches from high to low. Since the timer period in real time is the product of the timer clock period and the counting range of the timer, we can adjust the resolution of the PWM unit by choosing the proper combination of timer clock period and timer bit width. Pulse-width modulation can be implemented with a combination of hardware and software: two timers keep track of the PWM period and compare period; software is responsible for switching the PWM output value based on the states of the two timers.

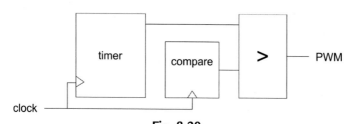

Fig. 8.20
Block diagram of a pulse-width modulation (PWM) unit.

Two characteristics are directly related to the design of the motor controller. **Motor speed accuracy** depends in part on the control algorithm but also depends on the accuracy of the sensing system used to measure the shaft RPM. We want the shaft rotation speed to be slow relative to the accuracy of the timer used to measure shaft speed; if the shaft rotates at a rate similar to the timer, small variations in shaft speed may result in large measurement errors. The **response time** measures the time between a command for a new speed and the time at which the motor achieves that speed within some specified accuracy. We can model response time as a step response and use classical control theory methods to design the controller from the response time specification.

The **H bridge** is widely used to control motors and to allow the power supply to be supplied to the motor in either polarity. The logical organization of the H bridge is shown in Fig. 8.21. It is a relative of the full-wave diode bridge used to rectify AC signals. The voltage across the middle of the H depends on the control signal values a, b of the four switches on the legs of the H. As shown in Fig. 8.22, setting $a=1$, $b=0$ applies the input voltage V to the bridge with the positive voltage on the left side. Setting $a=0$, $b=1$ reverses the polarity of the voltage on the bridge by reversing its connection to the input voltage. In some applications, we want to be able to disconnect the bridge from the input, so we do not necessarily require that $a=\bar{b}$.

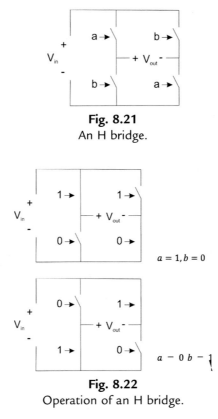

Fig. 8.21
An H bridge.

Fig. 8.22
Operation of an H bridge.

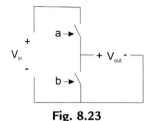

Fig. 8.23
A half H bridge circuit.

The **half H bridge**, shown in Fig. 8.23, is often used in power and drive circuits. As the name implies, it provides two switches that allow one connection to be switched between terminals with opposite polarities. In a motor application, an LC tank is typically added in series to the bottom loop to create oscillations when the motor is not connected to the high power supply voltage.

An H bridge IC combines the H bridge function with driver circuits that can provide the large currents required for inductive loads. The L298 [56] provides two H bridges. It operates at a supply voltage of up to 46 V and can supply DC output current up to 4 A. Its control inputs have a very high $V_{IL} = 1.5$ V, the maximum voltage that is considered a valid logic 0; this high voltage provides good noise immunity. The DRV8844 provides four half H bridges which can be configured in various combinations of half and full H bridges.

We will start with a brushed motor speed controller. As shown in Fig. 8.24, a brushed DC motor uses a **commutator** to chop the DC supply. Brushes connect the electromagnets to the commutator to supply alternating polarities. The switching state of the electromagnets is timed to attract to and repel from the poles of the permanent magnets to spin the shaft.

The motor speed controller application consists of three tasks: a control law task, a command input task, and a motor command output task.

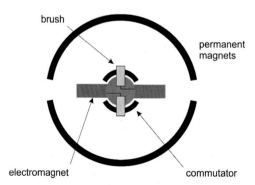

Fig. 8.24
A brushed DC motor.

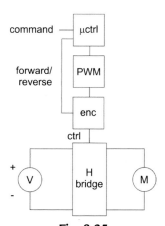

Fig. 8.25

An open-loop motor speed controller.

The simplest motor speed controller, shown in Fig. 8.25, operates open loop—it drives the motor based on a speed command without checking the actual speed of the motor. In this case, the control law maps a command speed to a PWM level. The control law can take one of several forms. The simplest open-loop control law is a linear function that maps the command speed to a PWM duty cycle value. However, the motor may not operate entirely linearly. We can create an open-loop control law to adjust for motor nonlinearities using either a functional description or table lookup.

The motor M is connected to its power supply V_M through an H bridge. We use the two control inputs a, b of the H bridge to both control the polarity of the motor voltage and to modulate its pulse width. If $a=b=0$, the motor will be disconnected from its power supply. We can use an encoder to turn the PWM duty cycle waveform into the H bridge control signals; a separate input determines whether the motor runs in forward or reverse.

If we allow the motor to operate in either direction, we need to be careful when we switch rotational directions. Commanding the H bridge to immediately from forward to reverse configuration can cause excessive transients that can damage components. We can design the logic of the H bridge encoder to provide a disconnected mode. We can then design the control law with short-term memory to insert a **dead zone** in between changes in direction.

The sample rate for the microcontroller should be fast relative to the top rotational speed of the motor.

Fig. 8.26 shows the block diagram for a closed-loop brushed motor speed controller. We use the microcontroller to execute the control law. It reads the shaft encoder at *sense* to monitor the speed of the motor.

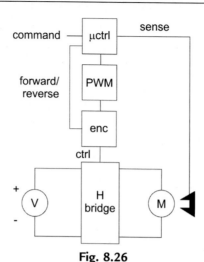

Fig. 8.26
A closed-loop brushed motor speed controller.

A typical software/hardware partition for the motor controller computes the control law in software, performs the PWM function primarily in hardware, and counts shaft rotation events in hardware.

We can sense the speed of the motor using the shaft encoder of Section 3.11. The number of divisions on the encoder disk determines the precision with which we can measure the shaft RPM.

We need to choose two parameters for the pulse-width modulation operation: the PWM period and the PWM duty cycle resolution. The period should be small relative to the time constant of the motor, which is determined by the motor's inductance and internal resistance. These parameters are not always provided on motor data sheets but they can be measured. The PWM period is typically short enough to allow several PWM periods in one revolution of the motor at its maximum speed.

The rate of shaft encoder pulses varies with the motor speed. Using a hardware counter to count the shaft pulses in an interval eliminates the interrupt handler overhead that would be required for each encoder pulse.

The control law sample rate should be high enough to provide proper tracking of the commanded speed. The sample rate in turn determines the required execution period T_{law} for the control law task. If we use an interrupt service routine to execute the control law, we can find the total task execution time as the combination of the interrupt response time and the control law function execution time:

$$C_{law} = t_{intr} + t_{ctrl}. \tag{8.12}$$

The total CPU utilization is then

$$U_{law} = \frac{t_{intr} + t_{ctrl}}{T_{law}}.$$
(8.13)

The numerical precision required for the control law function depends in part on the range of motor speeds at which the control system must operate. For a speed range $[R_{min}, R_{max}]$, the dynamic range of the values must be at least $\lceil \log_2(R_{max} - R_{min}) \rceil$. We must also take into account the controller gains, which increase the dynamic range to $\lceil \log_2 K_{pid}(R_{max} - R_{min}) \rceil$ where K_{pid} is the maximum of the three controller gains. Our control law does not include any division which helps to limit the required dynamic range. Many small microcontrollers support hardware floating-point operations. If the microcontroller does not support floating-point arithmetic, we can carefully design the code and the controller parameters to use entirely integer arithmetic. Multiplying and dividing by powers of two allows us to use bit-level operations as substitutes, although at the cost of reduced accuracy of the control law, since the parameters must be rounded to powers of two.

Brushless DC motors were made possible by high-speed power electronics. As shown in Fig. 8.27, a brushless motor does not have a mechanical commutator—it uses a controller to directly energize the coils of the motor [10]. The fixed magnets are on the motor shaft; the electromagnets push and pull relative to those magnets to spin the motor shaft. The figure shows a three-phase motor with two phases per coil. The three ABC leads allow each pair of coils to be separately energized. The controller must precisely time the coil energization. Directly controlling the coils allows the controller to more precisely control the position and speed of the shaft.

As with brushed motors, we use pulse-width modulation to regulate the motor speed. Whenever the PWM duty interval is active, we must provide the energizing signals to the coils

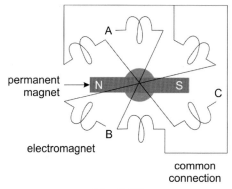

Fig. 8.27
A brushless DC motor.

at the appropriate times. Each phase of the **commutation period** T_C is used in both push and pull mode by applying positive and negative voltages.

Fig. 8.28 shows the timing of the drive signals for the brushless motor phases. The motor coils are configured as a Y circuit with a common connection. The connections for the three phases are labeled A, B, C. The positive energizing voltages are labeled H and the negative energizing voltages as L. Each phase also has an undriven dead time interval, shown in the figure as Z regions. Fig. 8.29 illustrates the operation of the motor at three times shown in the timing diagram. Switching the coils between high side and low side in the proper order provides a rotating magnetic field that pulls the rotor's permanent magnet around the motor.

As with the brushed DC motor, the pulse-width modulator signal is used as input to the decoder that controls the H bridge. But in this case, the code used to control the H bridge configuration is determined by the shaft position sensor. While we could use a shaft encoder, the motor itself provides sensing opportunities. In a **sensor-controlled brushless motor**, a set of Hall effect sensors are used to determine when the electromagnets pass known points. In a **sensorless brushless motor**, the back EMF produced by the motor can be used to determine its position. In this case, the back EMF is sensed as a voltage on an undriven terminal of the motor using an analog-digital converter. We can compare the back EMF to a reference voltage to generate a zero-crossing event.

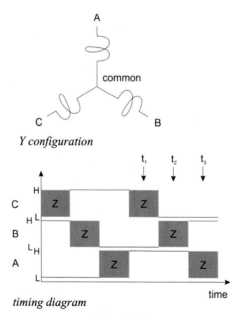

Fig. 8.28
Timing of drive signals in a brushless DC motor.

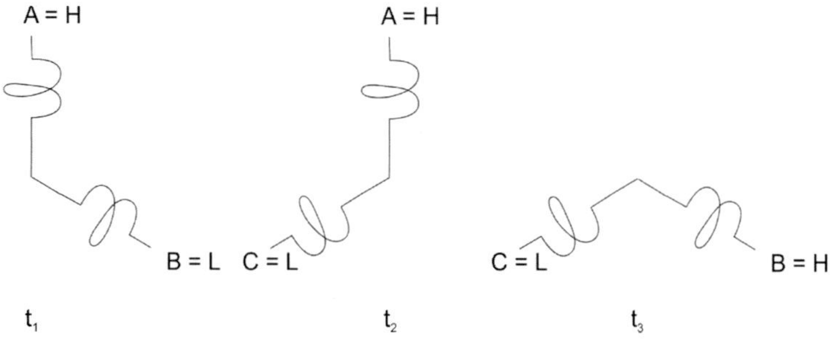

Fig. 8.29
Operation of a brushless motor over several commutation periods.

Brushless motor controllers must run at much higher rates than are required for brushed motor controllers—the motor must be actively controlled within fractions of a revolution. The commutation scheme of Fig. 8.28 changes configurations every 60 degrees, requiring a task period of $6 \times rev/s$.

Two tasks can be used to operate the motor. One task performs commutations that change which coils are energized. This task is controlled by a timer whose timeout interval is based on an estimate of the motor speed. Another task monitors zero crossings of the back EMF and performs control law calculations to update the commutation time. Zero crossings are handled as events. If the motor is spinning at the commanded speed, the zero crossing should occur at the middle of the commutation period. If the zero crossing occurs early, for example, the motor is running too slow and the commutation period needs to be shortened. A separate startup control algorithm is usually required to get the motor up to speed.

The rate at which the commutation and zero crossing tasks execute depends on motor speed. We can find the worst-case CPU utilization based on the minimum commutation period, which for a 60 degrees control scheme is equal to $T_{min} = 6/rev_{max}$. Given a commutation execution time t_c and zero crossing execution time t_z, the worst-case CPU utilization is

$$U_{brushless} = \frac{t_c + t_z}{T_{min}}. \tag{8.14}$$

A wide range of microcontrollers have been designed with brushless motor control in mind. The Microchip Technology PIC16F [37] includes an analog-digital converter, analog comparator, voltage reference, and multiple timers; it performs integer arithmetic. The TI TMS320F28004x microcontroller [71] uses a 32-bit CPU with floating-point arithmetic, a separate control law accelerator with floating-point arithmetic, three analog/digital converters, seven windowed comparators, and 16 extended PWM units.

Further Reading

Nisagara and Torres [44] and Brown [10, 11] discuss brushless DC motor control.

Questions

Q8.1   What must be added to the jack detector circuit of Section 5.14 to create a complete interface?

Q8.2   What must be added to the electret microphone amplifier circuit of Section 4.11 to create a complete interface?

Q8.3   We need to build an 8-tap digital filter with 16-bit data values to run at a rate of 40 kHz. Is an 8-bit, 32 MHz microcontroller with 256 bits of RAM likely to be able to implement the filter in software? Explain.

Q8.4   Which is likely to be a cheaper way to implement a two-pole low-pass filter: analog or digital programmable logic? Explain.

Appendix A: TTL Logic

A.1 Introduction

TTL logic [58] is based on bipolar transistors. TTL is less common today but the comparison to CMOS helps to underline why we need to adhere to certain specifications. Many different logic families have been created with different advantages and design characteristics.

A.2 TTL Logic Circuits

Fig. A.1 shows two types of bipolar transistors: NPN and PNP. The three terminals are known as the base, emitter, and collector. The base terminal of the bipolar transistor has a relatively low impedance, in contrast to the high gate impedance of the MOSFET used in CMOS logic.

Fig. A.2 shows the characteristic curve plot for an *npn* bipolar transistor. The plot shows the collector current as a function of emitter-collector voltage for a range of base currents. A minimum level of base current is required to turn on the transistor. Once the transistor is on, the collector current becomes largely a function of the base current. We will discuss bipolar transistor characteristics in more detail in Chapter 4.

Fig. A.3 shows a TTL inverter. We can understand its operation for two cases:

- When the input voltage is low, Q_1 turns on. It creates a flow of current out of Q_2's base. As a result, Q_2 is off. Current flows through R_2 to turn on Q_3, which pulls the output high. The output diode prevents reverse currents through the output stage.
- If the input voltage is high, current flows through Q_1's emitter to turn on Q_2. The current through R_3 provides a base-collector voltage to turn on Q_4, which pulls the output down.

The Q_3, Q_4 pair are known as a **totem pole** output circuit.

The TTL fanout problem is caused by limited current. Let's concentrate here on the case in which the driver transistor's output is a logic 1. A TTL gate can provide a maximum output current. It also requires a minimum input current. As we add more gates to the fanout, we divide the output current among more sinks. Eventually, none of the sink gates receive enough current to allow them to generate their correct outputs. In this case, the TTL circuit never produces the

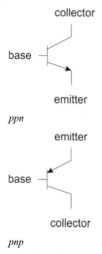

Fig. A.1
Bipolar transistors.

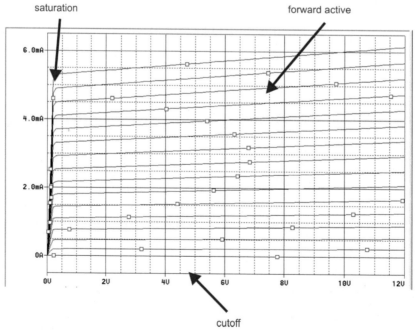

Fig. A.2
Characteristic curves for a bipolar transistor.

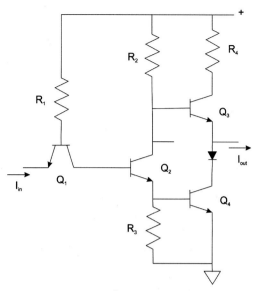

Fig. A.3
A TTL inverter.

V_{CC}	$4.5\ V \leq V_{CC} \leq 5.5\ V$
V_{IH}	2.0 V
V_{IL}	0.8 V
V_{OH}	2.7 V
V_{OL}	0.25 V
I_{IH}	0.1 mA
I_{IL}	−0.4 mA

Fig. A.4
Specifications for a TTL logic gate [38].

proper value; in contrast, the CMOS gates will eventually produce a valid output if we give them enough time.

Fig. A.4 gives specifications for a TTL logic gate, in this case a 74-series low-power Schottky gate. TTL logic is more sensitive to power supply voltage and the allowable range here is smaller than that for the CMOS gate. While the CMOS logic levels were fairly symmetric, the TTL logic levels are not, with the logic 1 voltage range much larger than the logic 0 voltage range.

A.3 High-Impedance and Open Outputs

In the case of TTL, a high impedance configuration is known as **open collector**. The maximum current supplied by the pullup resistor must be no larger than the maximum sink current of one gate and the current flowing from the inputs of the *n* fanout gates [58]:

$$R_L \geq \frac{V_{CC} - V_{OL}, \max}{I_{OL} - nI_{IL}} \qquad (A.1)$$

A.4 Example: Open-Collector and High-Impedance Busses

Busses are common connections that are used for data communication between various combinations of devices. Only one device at a time may write the bus. The destination for the data may be one or several devices. We can use two different circuit families to design busses with different characteristics.

We can use **pullup resistors** to build busses that allow easy connection and disconnection of devices. If the transistors used on the bus are bipolar, we refer to the bus as **open-collector**. A classic example of the open-collector bus is I_2C, which we discussed in Section 2.3.

Fig. A.5 shows an open-collector bus circuit. The bus is a wire connected to pullup resistor R_{pu}. Each module on the bus has a pulldown transistor Q_1, Q_2, etc. If any of the devices turns on its pulldown transistor, the bus voltage is pulled to a low voltage. If no modules are on, the bus is kept at a high voltage thanks to the pullup resistor. If two modules turn on their pulldown transistors, the bus continues to operate normally. Open-collector and open-drain busses are robust because they are insensitive to multiple devices writing on the bus. However, the pullup transistor causes the bus to be relatively slow.

Fig. A.6 shows a high-impedance bus. Consider first a bus that is only a wire without a pullup resistor. Each module uses a three-state gate to connect to the bus. (We use inverting gates here but the polarity of the bus logic is not important to its circuit characteristics.) If one three-state gate is enabled, it controls the value on the bus. If two three-state gates are enabled and they output the same value, the bus continues to operate. If the two gates have opposite values, they will fight each other, resulting in at least a bad logic value on the bus and perhaps damage to the circuits. If no three-state gate is enabled, the bus is floating and does not have a reliable digital

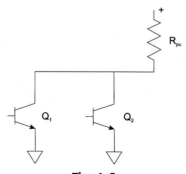

Fig. A.5
An open-collector bus.

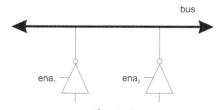

Fig. A.6
A high-impedance bus.

value. We can use a weak pullup to keep the bus at a valid logic value; the pullup is chosen to provide a small enough current that if a three-state gate can overcome it and determine the bus value.

Questions

QA.1 A TTL gate has a maximum output current of 16 mA and maximum input current of −1.6 mA. What is the maximum fanout of this gate when it drives other gates of the same type?

QA.2 A bipolar family has a maximum output current of 1.6 mA and minimum input current of 40 μA. What is the maximum fanout?

Appendix B: Bipolar Amplifiers

B.1 Introduction

Section B.2 develops models for bipolar transistors while Section 3.5 introduces standard circuit topologies for bipolar amplifiers. Section B.4 uses these models and circuits to analyze the design of a simple bipolar amplifier. Section B.5 works through the design of a two-stage amplifier.

B.2 Bipolar Transistor Models

The large current gain of bipolar transistors still find uses in amplifier design thanks to their large current gain.

Fig. B.1 shows a simple small signal model for a bipolar transistor. This form of the small signal model is known as the **pi model** due to the shape of the schematic. This model can be extended with additional resistors and capacitors to more accurately model some characteristics of the bipolar transistor. The base-emitter path is modeled as a resistance r_π. The collector-emitter path is modeled as a current source; it is shown as a diamond to indicate that its value is controlled by another parameter. The current produced by the collector-emitter current source depends on the voltage across the base-emitter resistor. The value g_m is the transconductance of the transistor, which relates the base-emitter voltage to the collector-emitter current. Since $\beta = g_m r_\pi$, an equivalent value for the current source is βi_b.

Fig. B.2 shows an alternate, equivalent model known as the **t model**. We can use standard circuit transformations to turn the pi model into the t model for and *vice versa*. The resistor r_e models the dependency between V_{BE} and I_B [5]:

$$r_e = \frac{kT}{qI_c} \approx \frac{kT}{qI_e} = \frac{26\,\text{mV}}{I_e}. \tag{B.1}$$

In this formula, k is Boltzmann's constant, T is temperature, and q is the charge of the electron.

Fig. B.3 gives some important parameters for a typical NPN transistor [20]. By convention, we use small letters for small-signal values and capital letters for DC values. Of particular interest

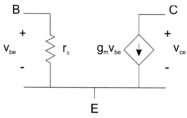

Fig. B.1
A small signal pi model for a bipolar transistor.

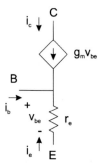

Fig. B.2
A small signal t model for a bipolar transistor.

h_{FE}	$min.\,20\ @\ V_{CE} = 1.0V, I_C = 1\,mA$
	$100 \leq h_{FE} \leq 300\ @\ V_{CE} = 1.0V, I_C = 10\,mA$
f_T	$min.\,300\ @\ V_{CE} = 20V, I_C = 10\,mA, f = 100\,MHz$

SPICE model:

NPN (Is=6.734f Xti=3 Eg=1.11 Vaf=74.03 Bf=416.4 Ne=1.259 Ise=6.734 Ikf=66.78m Xtb=1.5 Br=.7371 Nc=2
Isc=0 Ikr=0 Rc=1 Cjc=3.638p Mjc=.3085 Vjc=.75 Fc=.5 Cje=4.493p Mje=.2593 Vje=.75 Tr=239.5n Tf=301.2p
Itf=.4 Vtf=4 Xtf=2 Rb=10)

Fig. B.3
Selected data sheet entries for a bipolar transistor [20].

is h_{FE}, the DC current gain, which is another name for β. We will use the median value $h_{FE} = 200$ for our calculations. The value f_T is the **gain-bandwidth product**, the product of the small signal gain at some reference frequency and the transistor's -3 dB cutoff frequency. This data sheet also gives a SPICE model for the transistor. The parameters given by different manufacturers for a given type of component can vary; we may have to estimate the parameter we want based on the values we are given.

Large signal transistor models take into account the device characteristics over a wide range of voltages and currents. A bipolar transistor's operation is described by its **characteristic**

curve plot which gives I_C vs. V_{CE} as a set of characteristic curves, each at a different I_B operating point for the device. Operating curves are often measured experimentally using a **curve tracer** that applies sequences of swept voltages to the device and measures its response. We can use OrCAD and PSpice to simulate the operation of a curve tracer. Fig. B.4 shows the setup. The transistor's base is driven by a current source. We sweep two variables: the collector-emitter voltage and the base current. The resulting curves are shown in Fig. B.5.

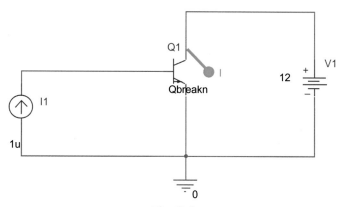

Fig. B.4
A curve tracer circuit for a bipolar transistor.

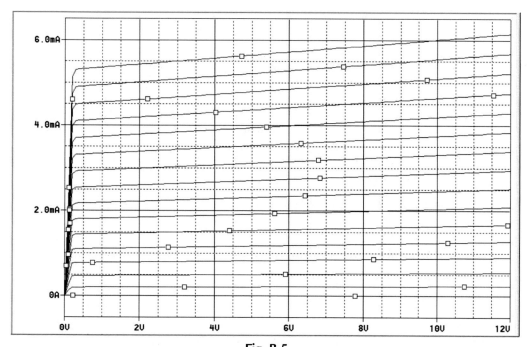

Fig. B.5
A simulated curve tracing of a bipolar transistor.

BJTs are described as having several different **operating regions**. The **cutoff region** corresponds to base voltages too low to turn on the base-emitter junction, the **saturation region** corresponds to very small collector-emitter voltages, and the **forward active region** gives a collector current that is approximately independent of the collector-emitter voltage.

One of the most basic parameters of a bipolar transistor is β, a measure of current gain:

$$\beta = \frac{I_B}{I_C}. \tag{B.2}$$

Bipolar transistors typically provide $\beta \approx 100-200$. Some data sheets may distinguish between DC and small-signal β. Some data sheets quote h_{FE}; while this parameter has a slightly different definition, for basic design purposes we can treat it as being equal to β at DC. h_{fe} is the small-signal version of h_{FE}.

The Ebers-Moll model [57] is a widely used model for bipolar transistors:

$$I_E = I_{FO}\left(e^{qV_{EB}/kT} - 1\right) - \alpha_I I_{FO}\left(e^{qV_{CB}/kT} - 1\right), \tag{B.3}$$

$$I_C = -\alpha_I I_{RO}\left(e^{qV_{EB}/kT} - 1\right) + I_{RO}\left(e^{qV_{CB}/kT} - 1\right). \tag{B.4}$$

The parameters I_{FO}, I_{RO} are the forward- and reverse-biased currents of the diodes formed by the transistor junctions; α_N, α_I are the fprward amd reverse common-base current gains.

We are primarily concerned with the BJT's behavior in the forward active region. Fig. B.6 signal gives a model for that region of operation. The collector current is equal to βI_B. The base current follows a diode law:

$$I_C = \frac{I_S}{\beta} e^{qV_{BE}/kT}. \tag{B.5}$$

The parameter I_S depends on several device parameters; for our purposes, it is sufficient to know that it is exponentially dependent on temperature.

B.3 Bipolar Amplifier Topologies

In this section, we will introduce the basic circuit topologies for low-power amplifier circuits using bipolar transistors. We can build three different circuit types out of a single transistor, each of which uses a different transistor terminal as its common connection between the input and output sides of the amplifier. Other topologies are also possible by using more than one transistor.

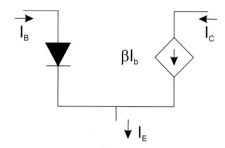

Fig. B.6
A large signal model for a bipolar transistor.

B.3.1 Common Emitter Amplifier

We can use several different circuit topologies to build bipolar amplifiers. Fig. B.7 shows the **common emitter** amplifier, so-called because the emitter is part of both the input and output current flows.

We can find the voltage gain of the common emitter amplifier by performing AC analysis on the circuit and substituting the bipolar small signal model for the device. Fig. B.8 shows the schematic for the model. The input source and power supply are reduced to shorts for AC analysis. We assume that the load resistance is disconnected. This gives the output voltage to fall across R_C. The resistance at the base is $g_m v_{be}$. Voltage gain is the ratio of output voltage to input voltage:

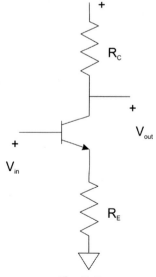

Fig. B.7
A common emitter amplifier.

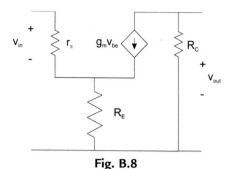

Fig. B.8
A small signal model for common emitter gain.

$$A_v = \frac{V_{ce}}{V_{be}}. \tag{B.6}$$

The output voltage is $V_{ce} = g_m V_{be} R_C = \beta i_b R_C$. The input voltage is due to the voltage drop across r_e which has two components: the drop across the input resistance which is a function of base current; and the drop across R_E which depends on the emitter current. The total input voltage is $V_{be} = (\beta+1)r_e + \beta I_b R_E$. Substituting,

$$A_v = \frac{g_m V_{be} R_C}{(\beta+1)r_e + \beta I_b R_E} \approx \frac{R_C}{R_E}. \tag{B.7}$$

B.3.2 Common Collector Amplifier

Fig. B.9 shows a **common collector** circuit, more commonly known as an **emitter follower**. It gives a voltage gain of 1 but it provides high current gain with the input and output signals in phase. The emitter follower is used when we want to *buffer* or separate a signal without requiring any voltage gain.

B.3.3 Common Base Amplifier

The **common base** amplifier is shown in Fig. B.10. It has a low input impedance and high output impedance. It provides a current gain of 1.

B.3.4 Cascode Amplifier

While the common base configuration is uncommon, the **cascode** amplifier of Fig. B.11 is widely used. It uses a pair of transistors to create two stages: the first stage is in the common emitter configuration while the second stage is in the common base configuration. This amplifier provides good signal gain, good bandwidth, and high impedance for both the input and output. Without going into too much detail, this presence of the common base stage reduces

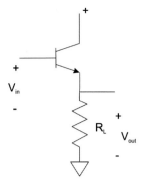

Fig. B.9

A common collector or emitter follower circuit.

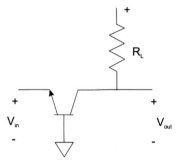

Fig. B.10

A common base amplifier.

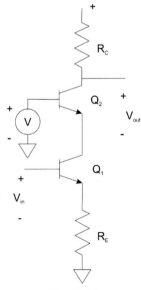

Fig. B.11

A cascode amplifier.

the effect of the parasitic coupling between the base and collector in the first stage transistor, thereby providing strong gain at higher frequencies than would be possible from a simple common emitter amplifier.

B.3.5 Differential Amplifier

A bipolar **differential amplifier**, also known as the **differential pair**, is shown in Fig. B.12. The current through $Q_1 + Q_2$ is constant; differences in the input voltages V_+, V_- result in amplified differences in the output voltages V_1, V_2.

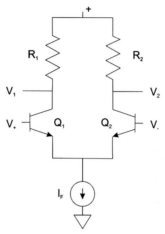

Fig. B.12
A bipolar differential amplifier.

B.3.6 Current Sources

The differential amplifier makes use of a current source. A practical circuit that provides a circuit independent of load is useful in many amplifiers and other circuits. Fig. B.13 shows a basic current source built with a bipolar transistor. The voltage divider provides a base voltage for the bipolar transistor that governs its collector-emitter current. This circuit is adequate for simple applications but is prone to several problems: variations in the power supply voltage will cause variations in the output current; temperature variations will cause the transistor β to change, resulting in a change in the output current; inaccuracies in the resistor values will cause an unanticipated output current.

A **current mirror** is used to copy an input current to an output current while isolating the input from the output. Current mirrors are designed with low input impedance to minimize input voltage variations; they provide high output impedance to reduce variations caused by the load. Several current mirror circuits have been designed; one example is the Widlar current mirror of Fig. B.14. Accurate current mirrors require matched transistors so building one out of discrete

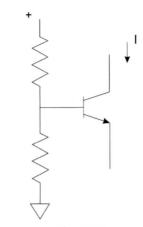

Fig. B.13
A simple bipolar current source.

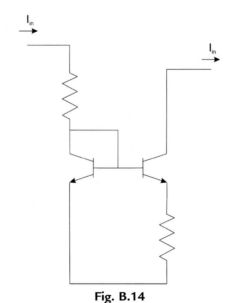

Fig. B.14
A Widlar current mirror using bipolar transistors.

transistors may be counterproductive. Several integrated circuit current mirrors are available that take advantage of the good matching characteristics of ICs.

B.4 Low-Power Bipolar Amplifiers

We have two primary requirements for an amplifier: its voltage gain A_V and the current it can deliver for a given load impedance. We also have some requirements on the minimum frequency of operation of the amplifier.

Given a circuit topology for the amplifier, we can derive several models for different analytical purposes. We use a load line to determine the current through the output stage transistors. Based on that calculation, we derive the values for the passive components.

B.4.1 Bipolar Amplifier Models

To make the common emitter amplifier of Fig. B.15 work in practice, we need a few more components. This schematic includes some biasing and other interfacing circuits around the core of the common emitter, which consists of the output transistor Q_1 and the output resistor

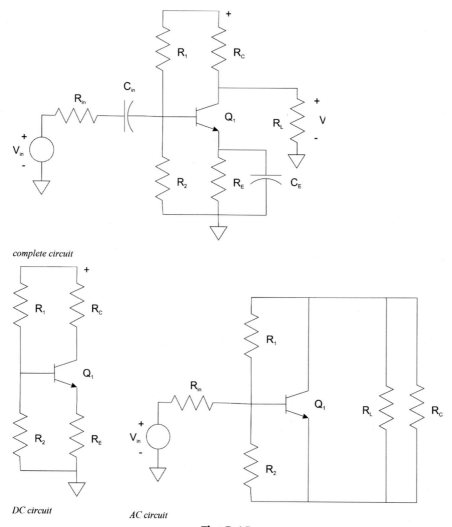

complete circuit

DC circuit *AC circuit*

Fig. B.15
A common emitter amplifier with associated circuitry.

R_E. The figure shows three versions of the circuit: the full circuit with biasing and other components, the DC circuit with capacitors treated as open circuits, and the AC circuit with capacitors and the power supply treated as short circuits.

B.4.2 Load Line Analysis

The transistor in isolation can operate at many different combinations of voltages and currents. We can constrain our analysis by putting it into a circuit. Fig. B.16 shows the **load line** for a common emitter amplifier. The load resistor R_L restricts the possible set of voltages and currents across and through the transistor: Kirchoff's current law tells us that $I_R = I_{CE}$; Kirchoff's voltage law tells us that $V_R + V_{CE} = V_{CC}$. The load line intercepts the y-axis where $V_{CE} = 0$ and the current depends entirely on the load transistor: $I_{CE} = V_{CC}/R_L$. It intercepts the x-axis when there is no collector-emitter current, namely, V_{CC}.

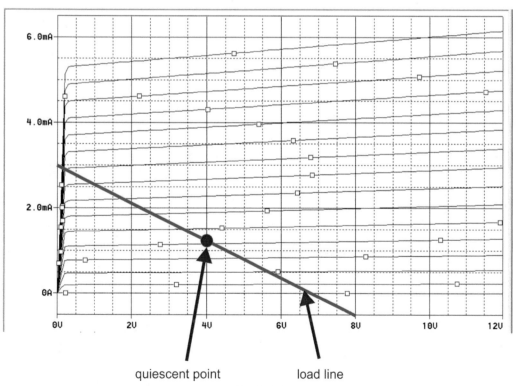

Fig. B.16
A load line for a bipolar common emitter amplifier.

B.4.3 Large Signal Analysis

We can now consider large signal analysis to choose the values of the remaining components. To choose the component values for the resistors and capacitors in this amplifier, we need to take into account the transistor characteristics. The value of V_{CE} follows the load line thanks to R_3 and R_4:

$$V_{CE} = V_{CC} - I_C R_3 - I_E R_4 \approx V_{CC} - I_C(R_3 + R_4). \tag{B.8}$$

The collector and emitter current are related by the parameter α which is close to 1. As we change the base current, the amplifier moves up and down the load line.

The x-axis intercept for the load line is given by the power supply voltage V_{CC}. We want to choose a power supply voltage that is bigger than the maximum voltage swing we require for the output; we are usually restricted to a few standard available output voltages from our power supply. The y-axis intercept is found by assuming that the voltage across R_L is equal to the full power supply voltage:

$$I_{C0} = \frac{V_{CC}}{R_L}. \tag{B.9}$$

We will not run the load at this maximum voltage, however. As we move toward very low V_{CE} values, the transistor falls out of saturation and eventually turns off. The load line is only an approximation at both ends of the scale.

B.4.4 Component Value Formulas

Let's now use the DC circuit to derive the resistor voltages. R_1, R_2 act as a *voltage divider* to set the DC voltage at the base of Q_1. We can choose the voltage we want to use at this point; that selection will define a point on the load line known as the **quiescent point**. We will choose a quiescent point halfway between ground and V_{CC}. That choice means gives us this formula for the voltage divider:

$$\frac{V_{CC}}{2} = V_{CC} \frac{R_2}{R_1 + R_2}. \tag{B.10}$$

This formula tells us that $R_1 = R_2$ but does not fully specify the resistor values; in many design problems, the component values are underspecified and we use several different criteria to come up with final values. One rule of thumb is that the current through R_1, R_2 should be about ten times larger than the base current. Since $I_B = I_C/\beta$, if we assume that $\beta = 100$, then

$$I_{R1R2} = \frac{I_{C0}}{10} = \frac{V_{CC}}{R_1 + R_2}. \tag{B.11}$$

Given that $R_1 = R_2$,

$$R_1 = R_2 = \frac{I_{C0}}{5V_{CC}}.$$ (B.12)

The role of R_E is to provide negative feedback to stabilize the amplifier against temperature-dependent effects. If the collector current goes up, for example, because the transistor heats up and so produces more current, then the voltage drop across R_E will go up. This means that the base-collector current goes down, which means that the base current goes down, which means that Q_1's output current goes down, correcting the problem.

The values for R_c and R_E are also underspecified. One common heuristic is to choose the values by splitting the power supply equally among R_C, R_E, and V_{CE}. This gives

$$R_c = R_E = \frac{V_{CC}}{3I_{C0}}.$$ (B.13)

We also need to find values for the two capacitors. C_E shorts R_E at high frequencies. We do not need to stabilize the amplifier at high frequencies, only DC. Shorting out R_E increases the AC gain of the amplifier.

We use the -3 dB point of the RC combination as the transition frequency. Given a capacitor C and resistor R, the -3 dB point occurs at

$$X_C = 0.414R.$$ (B.14)

We saw in Section 1.6 that the reactance of a capacitive component is a function of frequency. The -3 dB frequency in Hertz is

$$f_{-3\,\text{dB}} = \frac{2.42}{2\pi RC}.$$ (B.15)

The resistance of importance for the value of C_E is the transistor's internal emitter resistance r_e. Its formula in EQ B.1-re depends on kT/q. At room temperature, $r_e = 26/I_C$. We can estimate I_C as the small signal emitter current I_e.

Given a cutoff frequency f_0 for the amplifier, we can choose $C_E = R_E$ at that frequency:

$$C_E = \frac{1}{2\pi f_0 r_E}.$$ (B.16)

In the case of C_{in}, we want to choose its value based on the parallel combination of R_1, R_2:

$$C_{in} = \frac{1}{2\pi f (R_1 \| R_2)}.$$ (B.17)

B.5 Driving a Low-Impedance Load Using Bipolar Amplifiers

We can use the basic amplifier circuits to build a two-stage amplifier designed to drive a low-impedance load using bipolar transistors.

This example gives us the chance to consider some practicalities. While we may calculate particular values for our components, we can't procure components with those exact values. Resistors, inductors, and capacitors all come in standard values. Those values are chosen to provide a good range of values and avoid gaps in coverage. Nonetheless, we must make use of the available values, which is one reason to design robust circuits that are tolerant of variations.

Beyond choosing fixed values, we must take into account the fact that passive components are manufactured to certain tolerances. For example, a 47 kΩ resistor with a tolerance of $\pm 10\%$ could have an actual value ranging from 42.3 to 5.17 kΩ. Components are generally available in several different tolerances; tighter tolerances cost more money.

Passive components are also given maximum power ratings. A component should not be operated at a power level higher than its rating. In general, some amount of headroom should be left in the power rating. Given the variation of component values and other operating conditions, devices operating at close to their rated power level may occasionally exceed that level, causing reliability problems.

Fig. B.17 shows the OrCAD schematic for the two-stage amplifier. The first stage uses Q_1 in a common-emitter configuration; the second stage uses Q_2 as an emitter follower. The amplifier is designed around a 12 V power supply. Our specifications include a voltage gain $A_v = -5$ and the ability to drive an 8 Ω load, which is the typical impedance for a large speaker (smaller speakers generally have a 4 Ω impedance). The amplifier should work over the standard

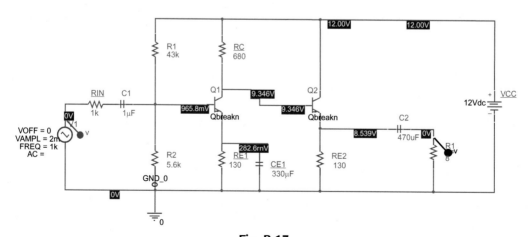

Fig. B.17
A two-stage bipolar amplifier.

audio range of $[f_L, f_H] = [100 \text{ Hz}, 20 \text{ kHz}]$. We assume that the impedance of the source is 1 kΩ. We can choose the component values starting at the input and, for the most part, move through to the output. We will simulate the circuit using the transistor model we used in Section B.2-bjt-model.

The first stage will supply all of the voltage gain for the amplifier. Given that we use the second stage for current amplification, we have some freedom in how we choose the collector current, so we choose a value of $I_C = 5$ mA.

We also want to choose the quiescent point voltage for Q_1, which we want to be near the middle of the power supply range. Fig. B.18 shows the load line based on the transistor curves, the power supply voltage, and the chosen collector current. We choose $V_{EQ1} = 8$ V as an operating point.

We use the voltage gain and collector current to determine the values for R_C and R_{E1}. The power supply voltage is dropped across the series combination of R_C, the collector-emitter region of Q_1, and R_{E1}. This gives $R_C + R_{E1} = (V_{CC} - V_{EQ1})/I_{C1}$. We know that for a common emitter configuration,

$$A_v \approx -\frac{R_C}{R_E}. \tag{B.18}$$

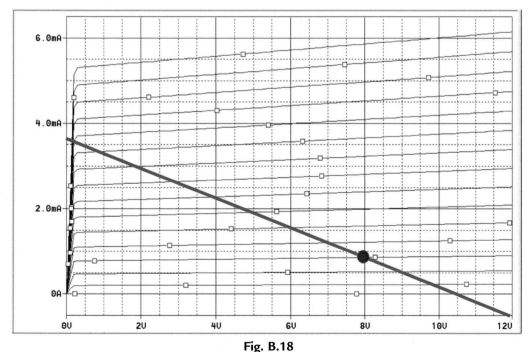

Fig. B.18
Load line for the first stage of the two-stage amplifier.

This gives us $R_C = 5R_{E1}$. When we combine this with the formula for $R_C + R_{E1}$, we find that $R_{E1} = 130\,\Omega$. As a result, $R_C = 650\,\Omega$ which we approximate as $680\,\Omega$. When we substitute these rounded values into the gain formula, we find that we should expect a voltage gain of 5.2.

The resistors R_1 and R_2 are the bias network for Q_1. They form a voltage divider to set the base voltage for Q_1: their ratio determines the bias voltage while their sum determines the current running through the bias circuit. We want the bias network to supply enough current that changes in Q_1 do not cause enough variation in the current flowing through R_1 and R_2 to change the bias voltage. This condition is satisfied when $R_1 \| R_2 \ll h_{FE}R_{E1}$. The transistor's amplification causes the resistance at its emitter to be seen through the base with an effective impedance amplified by h_{FE}. A good rule of thumb is that the bias network current should be $10\times$ the base current. The base current, in turn, is determined by the collector current. As a result, $I_B = I_C/h_{FE} = 25\,\mu\text{A}$. We therefore want the 12 V power supply to produce $10I_B = 250\,\mu\text{A}$ through the series combination of R_1 and R_2. As a result, $R_1 + R_2 = 48\,\text{k}\Omega$. The voltage across $R_2 = V_{12}/I_{R12}$ equals the sum of the voltage across R_{E1} and the transistor's base-emitter voltage of 0.7 V: $R_2 = (V_{BE} + I_{C1}R_{E1})/I_{R12} = 5400\,\Omega$ which we round to $5.6\,\text{k}\Omega$ As a result, $R_1 = 42.6\,\text{k}\Omega$ which we round to $43\,\text{k}\Omega$.

We choose the value of $C1$ to provide a 3 dB rolloff at our $f_L = 100$ Hz; this capacitance is in series with RIN. The impedance of a series RC is

$$Z = R + \frac{1}{sC}. \tag{B.19}$$

At high frequencies, the capacitor is a short and this equation reduces to $Z = R$. We want to find a value of C such that a frequency of $s = 2\pi f_L$, the magnitude of the RC impedance is $|Z(2\pi f_L)| = R\sqrt{2}$. The magnitude of the impedance is

$$|Z| = \sqrt{R^2 + \frac{1}{(sC)^2}}. \tag{B.20}$$

Substituting, we find that

$$C = \frac{1}{2\pi R f_L}. \tag{B.21}$$

In our case, $C1 = 8\,\mu\text{F}$.

We want to choose $CE1$ to roll off at our cutoff frequency f_L. In this case, our target is

$$\sqrt{2}\frac{R_c}{r_e} = \frac{R_c}{X_E}. \tag{B.22}$$

Substituting the formula for the parallel impedance of $CE1$ and r_e,

$$X_E = \frac{r_e}{\sqrt{2}} = \frac{1}{\sqrt{\frac{1}{r_e^2} + (sCE1)^2}}. \tag{B.23}$$

Solving for $CE1$,

$$CE1 = \frac{1}{2\pi f r_e}. \tag{B.24}$$

$r_e = 5\ \Omega$ and substituting into EQ B.24-ce1-3, we find a value of 318 μF which we round to 330 μF.

The second stage does not need a bias network because the first stage output maintains a reasonable operating voltage for Q_2. We choose a quiescent voltage of $V_{CEQ} = 8$ V and collector current of $I_{CQ} = 30$ mA. The emitter resistor $R_{E2} = (V_{CC} - V_{CEQ})/I_{CQ} = 133\ \Omega$ which we approximate as 130 Ω.

We set the value of C2 to provide an appropriate rolloff frequency given the load resistance of 8 Ω, giving us $C2 = 470$ μF.

Fig. B.19 shows the input and output waveforms for this amplifier. The simulation results show the actual gain to be about $A_V = 4.5$, somewhat lower than the estimated value.

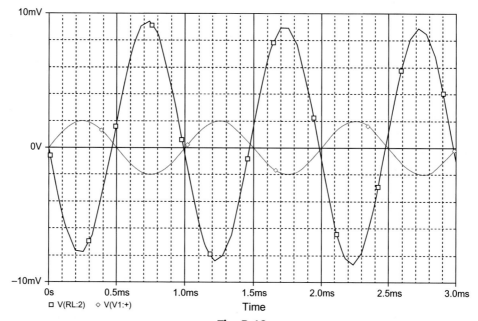

Fig. B.19
Input and output waveforms for the two-stage bipolar amplifier.

Questions

QB.1   A bipolar transistor has $\beta = 150$, $r_\pi = 4\ \Omega$. What is its g_m?

QB.2   You are given this curve tracing for a bipolar transistor:

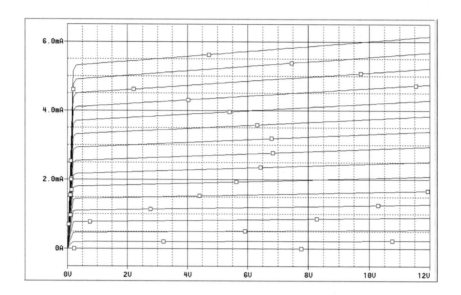

At approximately what value of V_{CE} does the transistor saturate?

QB.3   Draw a schematic for a small signal pi model of an emitter follower amplifier.

QB.4   A bipolar transistor has $\beta = 150$, $r_e = 5\ \Omega$. Find its small signal gain when used in a common emitter configuration with $R_C = 1\ k\Omega$, $R_E = 250\ \Omega$.

QB.5   In the differential amplifier of Fig. B.12,
$V_{CC} = 10\,\text{V}, R_1 = R_2 = 1\,k\Omega, g_{m1} = g_{m2} = 0.05\,\frac{A}{V}, I_F = 10\,\text{mA}$. Plot $V_{12} = V_1 - V_2$ with $V_+ = 2$ V and $1.9\ \text{V} \leq V_- \leq 2.1$ V.

QB.6   You are given this common emitter amplifier with $V_{CC} = 12$ V:

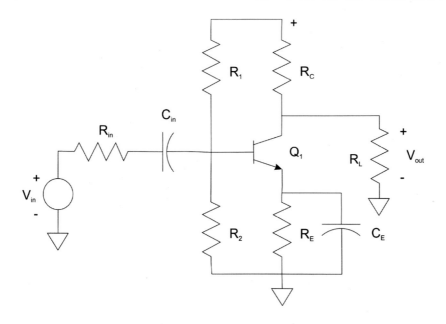

Choose R_1, R_2 to give a DC base voltage $V_{BE1} = 5$ V and a current through the resistors $I_{12} = 50$ mA.

References

[1] J. Adams, Headset/Radio Auto Sensing Jack, U. S. Patent 6,594,366, July 15, 2003.

[2] T. Allag, W. Liu, Battery-charging considerations for high-power portable devices, Analog Appl. J. 2014. Texas Instruments, 2Q.

[3] Altera, Thermal management, July 30, 2012. http://www.altera.com/support/devices/power/thermal/pow-thermal.html.

[4] Analog Devices, Chapter 11: The current mirror, August 20, 2017. https://wiki.analog.com/university/courses/electronics/text/chapter-11.

[5] ARRL, The ARRL Handbook for Radio Communications, 95th ed., ARRL, Newington, CT, 2018.

[6] T.P. Baker, A. Shaw, The cyclic executive model and Ada, in: Proceedings, Real-Time Systems Symposium, IEEE, 1998, pp. 120–129.

[7] J.R. Black, Electromigration—a brief survey and some recent results, in: IEEE Trans. Electron Devices 16 (4) (1969) 338–347.

[8] G.M.B.H. Robert Bosch, Automotive Electrics Automotive Electronics, fifth ed., Bentley Publishers, Cambridge, MA, 2007.

[9] C.W. Brokish, M. Lewis, A-Law and mu-Law Companding Implementations Using the TMS320C54x, Digital Signal Processing Solutions, Texas Instruments, 1997. SPRA163A.

[10] W. Brown, Brushless DC Motor Control Made Easy, Microchip Technology, 2002. AN857.

[11] W. Brown, Sensorless 3-Phase Brushless Motor Control With the PIC16FXXX, Microchip Technology, 2009. AN1305.

[12] J. Caldwell, Single-supply, electret microphone pre-amplifier reference design, Texas Instruments, TIDU765, 2015.

[13] Cirrus Logic, WM9801 Mono DAC With 2.6W Class AB/D Speaker Driver, Dynamic Range Controller and ReTuneTM Mobile Parametric Equalizer, Revision 4.0, 2016.

[14] Compaq, Hewlett-Packard, Intel, Lucent, Microsoft, NEC, Philips, Universal serial bus specification, revision 2.0, 27, 2000.

[15] T.R. Crompton, Battery Reference Book, third ed., Newnes, Oxford, 2000.

[16] Cypress, PSoC 5LP: CY8C52LP Family Datasheet, 001-84933, Revision L, June 13, 2017.

[17] G. Daryanani, Principles of Active Network Synthesis and Design, John Wiley and Sons, New York, 1976.

[18] Fairchild Semiconductor, BS170/MMBF170 n-Channel Enhancement Mode Field Effect Transistor, 1995.

[19] Fairchild Semiconductor, LM555 Single Timer, Revision 1.1.0, 2002.

[20] Fairchild Semiconductor, 2n3904 NPN General Purpose Amplifier, 2001.

[21] S. Farahani, Zigbee Wireless Networks and Transceivers, Newnes, Amsterdam, 2008.

[22] G.F. Franklin, J. David Powell, M.L. Workman, Digital Control of Dynamic Systems, third ed., Ellis-Kagle Press, Half Moon Bay, CA, 1998. Reprinted 2010.

[23] J. Haartsen, Bluetooth—the universal radio for *ad hoc*, wireless connectivity, Ericsson Rev. 3 (1998) 110–117.

[24] E. Hare, The ARRL RFI Book, ARRL, 1998.

[25] R. Heydon, Bluetooth Low Energy: The Developer's Handbook, Prentice Hall, Upper Saddle River, NJ, 2013.

[26] Hewlett-Packard Company, Intel Corporation, Microsoft Corporation, Renesas Corporation, ST-Ericsson, Texas Instruments, Universal Serial Bus 3.1 Specification, Revision 1.0, July 26, 2013.

[27] IBM International Technical Support Organization, Building Smarter Planet Solutions With MQTT and IBM WebSphere MQ Telemetry, Redbooks, September, 2012.

[28] Z. Shelby, K. Hartke, C. Bormann, The Constrained Application Protocol (CoAP), Internet Engineering Task Force RFC 7252, June, 2014.

[29] International Rectifier, "Designing practical high performance Class D audio amplifier, undated," Available from http://www.irf.com/product-info/audio.

[30] Jameco, TO-220 Data Sheet, Part No. BK-T220-0022-02, undated.

[31] D. Jarman, A Brief Introduction to Sigma Delta Conversion, Intersil, 1995. AN9504.

[32] W.G. Jung, IC Op-Amp Cookbook, third ed., Upper Saddle River, NJ, Prentice Hall PTR, 1997.

[33] D. Lancaster, Lancaster's Active Filter Cookbook, second ed., 1996. Newnes, New York.

[34] Linear Technology, LTC3780 High Efficiency, Synchronous, 4-Switch Buck-Boost Controller, 2005.

[35] LoRa Alliance, Technical Committee, LoRaWAN™ 1.1 Specification, version 1.1, October 11, 2017.

[36] Maxim Integrated, DC-DC Converter Tutorial, Tutorial 2031, November 29, 2001.

[37] Microchip Technology Inc., PIC16F/LF1824/1828 Data Sheet, 14/20-Pin Flash Microcontrollers with nanoWatt XLP Technology, Preliminary, DS4149A, 2010.

[38] Motorola, SN54/74LS04 Hex Inverter, undated.

[39] J.H. McClellan, R.W. Schaefer, M.A. Yoder, DSP First, second ed., Pearson, 2015.

[40] National Semiconductor, LM340/LM78MXX Series 3-Terminal Positive Regulators, DS007781, 2000.

[41] National Semiconductor, Op amp circuit collection, Application Note 31, 2002.

[42] National Semiconductor, LM380 2.5W Audio Power Amplifier, 2000.

[43] Nichibo Taiwan Corporation, RF-500TB-12560-R-S Nichibo DC motor, September 28, 2013.

[44] B. Nisagara, D. Torres, *Sensored 3-Phase BLDC* Motor Control *Using MSP430*, SLAA503, Texas Instruments, 2011.

[45] NXP Semiconductors, UM10204, I^{2}C-Bus Specification and User Manual, Rev. 03, 19 June, 2007.

[46] NXP Semiconductors, S32V234 Data Sheet, Document Number S22V234, Rev. 4, 2017.

[47] Philips Semiconductors, *I2S bus specification*, 1986. Revised June 5, 1996.

[48] B. Razavi, The current-steering DAC, IEEE Solid-State Circuits Mag. (2018) 11–15. Witner.

[49] Rubycon Corporation, Technical Notes for Electrolytic Capacitor, undated.

[50] D. Sauvageau, How (and why) we test USB power adapters, Tom's Hardware, 2018. January 21, http://www.tomshardware.com/reviews/usb-power-adapters-testing,5328.html.

[51] G.M. Sessler, J.E. West, Electrostatic Transducer, U. S. Patent 3,118,979, January 21, 1964.

[52] D.P. Siewiorek, R.S. Swarz, The Theory and Practice of Reliable System Design, Digital Press, 1982.

[53] C. Simpson, Characteristics of Rechargeable Batteries, SNAV533. Texas Instruments, 2011.

[54] C. Simpson, Battery Charging, SNAV557, Texas Instruments, 2011.

[55] R.J. Smith, R.C. Dorf, Circuits, Devices, and Systems: A First Course in Electrical Engineering, fifth ed., John Wiley and Sons, 1991.

[56] ST Microelectronics, L298 Dual Full-Bridge Driver, 2000.

[57] S.M. Sze, Physics of Semiconductor Devices, second ed., John Wiley and Sons, New York, 1981.

[58] Texas Instruments (Ed.), The TTL Data Book for Design Engineers, second ed., Texas Instruments Incorporated, 1987.

[59] Texas Instruments, *Precise Tri-Wave Generation*, SNOA854, Previously *National Semiconductor Linear Brief 23*, 1986.

[60] Texas Instruments, μA741, μA741Y General-Purpose Operational Amplifiers, 1970. SLOS094B, Revised September 2000.

[61] Texas Instruments, Op Amp and Comparators—Don't Confuse Them, 2001. SLOA067.

[62] Texas Instruments, 74AC11000 Quadruple 2-Input Positive-NAND Gate, 1987. SCLS054B, Revised June 2005.

[63] Texas Instruments, AN-263 Sine Wave Generation Techniques, SNOA665C, 2013.

[64] Texas Instruments, TPA6138A2 DirectPath™ Headphone Driver with Adjustable Gain, SLOS704B, 2015.

[65] Texas Instruments, TPA6166A2 3.5mm Jack Detect and Headset Interface IC, SLAS997B, revised January, 2015.

[66] Texas Instruments, LM555 Timer, SNAS548D, 2015.

[67] Texas Instruments, Switching Regulator Fundamentals, SNVA559A, 2016.

[68] Texas Instruments, *TAS6424L-Q1 27-W, 2-MHz Digital Input 4-Channel Automotive Class-D Audio Amplifier With Load-Dump Protection and I2C Diagnostics*, SLOS809, 2017.

[69] Texas Instruments, *TPA6464-01 50-W, 2-MHz Analog Input-Channel Automotive Class-D Audio Amplifier With Load Dump Protection and I2C Diagnostics*, SLOS995, 2017.

[70] Texas Instruments, LM386 Low Voltage Audio Power Amplifier, SNAS545C, revised May, 2017.

[71] Texas Instruments, TMS320F28004x Piccolo™ Microcontrollers, SPRS945C, revised December 2017, 2017.

[72] TT Electronics, Reflective Object Sensor: OPB703 through OPB705, OPB703WZ through OPB705WZ, OPB703AWZ through OPB705AWZ, 2016.

[73] J.F. Wakerly, Digital Design: Principles and Practices, fourth ed., Pearson, 2005.

[74] M. Wolf, The Physics of Computing, Morgan Kaufman, San Francisco, 2017.

[75] S. Wong, Dynamic power management for faster, more efficient battery charging, Analog Appl. J. (2013). Texas Instruments, 4Q.

Index

Note: Page numbers followed by *f* indicate figures.